Across the Everglades

A Canoe Journey of Exploration By Hugh L. Willoughby

Ex-Lieutenant Commanding Rhode Island Naval Reserve

Illustrated from Photographs
Taken by the Author

Fifth Edition

FLORIDA CLASSICS LIBRARY
Port Salerno, Florida

TO

THE NEW YORK
YACHT CLUB

TO WHOSE INTEREST IN ORIGINAL

GEOGRAPHICAL RESEARCH

THE PUBLICATION

OF THIS

RECORD OF A WINTER'S WORK

IN FLORIDA IS DUE

PREFACE

IF the reader has the patience and fortitude to follow me in my wanderings, he will perhaps find many preconceived and erroneous impressions of the character of the Everglades dissipated. I have elsewhere stated the purpose of my winter's work. It remains, then, only for me to thank those who have kindly aided me. I beg here to express my great indebtedness to my friend, Mr. H. M. Flagler, for the courtesies of his railroad and the special interest shown by him in the successful issue of my undertaking. I have also to thank Mr. J. I. Ingraham for loaning me the complete and interesting notes made by him during his own expedition. The vocabulary in this volume was greatly enriched by the use of that charming little book, " The Seminoles of Florida," by Minnie Moore Willson, enabling me to add much to my own stock of words.

Preface

For the analysis of the water of the Everglades I am indebted to the Harrison Laboratory of the University of Pennsylvania. Many of my negatives of Indians having been over-exposed, I have substituted the portraits of Matlo, Dr. Tiger, and Miami Doctor's Boy, which are from the camera of Commodore Ralph Munroe.

Hugh L. Willoughby.

"The Chalet," Newport, R. I.,
September, 1897.

Table of Contents

🐾

CHAPTER I

Table of Contents

CHAPTER V

List of Illustrations

List of Illustrations

ACROSS THE EVERGLADES

❧

CHAPTER I

Florida Geographically—The Everglades—The Seminole War—Characteristics of the Tribe—Previous Explorations.

THIS journey was undertaken in order to explore that unknown portion of the Everglades into which the Seminole Indians were driven during the Indian War, and which was left untouched by the two previous expeditions ; also to examine the fauna and flora of the region in the interests of the University of Pennsylvania. Its simple record may help to while away an idle hour for those who love an out-door life, and to whom the memories of the camp-fire are dear.

Florida was ceded to the United States by Spain, in the year 1821, in payment of damages done to our commerce by that country, which had been estimated at five million dollars.

Across the Everglades

Being our most southerly State, and touching a semitropical climate, it has naturally excited much interest from time to time from the settler, the seeker after health, the naturalist, and the sportsman who finds a variety of game in its thick, jungle-like hammocks, and a countless number of fish in its streams and around its sinuous coast. Every one is of course familiar with the general outline of the State; but many of us are surprised when we are told that Florida has twelve hundred miles of coast-line.

The warm water supplied by the Gulf of Mexico on the west and the Gulf Stream on the southeast (which at a few points almost laps the shore), in connection with the warm air in the southern portion of the State and the crystalline purity of the salt water in this latitude, make the conditions for the rapid propagation of marine life almost perfect.

It is a very interesting thing to trace through the various maps of many years ago the gradual evolution of the map we have to-day. From the very start, not only the interior has been incorrectly put down, but the coast has been from time to time changed by what was the guess-work alone of the geographers of the day, one copying the errors of the other, until it was difficult for our Department of the Interior to get reliable data with which to make its official map, and even this map cannot be relied upon very accurately in the extreme South. Our latest geodetic coast survey chart is really the only one to-day that we can look to to give the outline of the State as it exists, and the funds at the disposal of the Survey made it impossible to do any detailed work further than the outlying edge of regions like, for instance, the Ten Thousand Island Archipelago. The geographical knowledge of 1731 is very well shown in the accompanying reproduction of a map from " Histoire de la Conquête de la Floride," by Ferdinand de Soto, published in that year. Surely the coast-lines could not have changed so materially since that time.

The greatest error in this map seems to be in the width of the central portion of the State. Cape Canaveral could have afforded no shelter against a norther in those days, as it does to-day, unless there was a passage running back of the very large island, which is charted running east and west. The most interesting map, however, that in my search for early geography I have discovered, is one published in France in 1750. This map was accidentally found while on a visit to his family in France two years ago by a French gentleman now living in South Florida, and through his kindness I have reproduced it.

According to this map Florida was wedge-shaped, and a wonderfully mountainous country, the high peaks extending almost to the extreme South. Now, very strange to say, until recently our knowledge of the interior of the southern part was about as limited as that of the early French explorers ; for that portion is covered by the great Everglades, many parts of which the foot of a white man has never trod. Ever since the Indians were driven to the far South by the troops during the Seminole War, this land, or rather water, for there is certainly more water than land, has been deemed impenetrable. The very settlers along the edge of the east coast know absolutely nothing of what exists ten miles west of their farms.

It is without doubt the peculiar character of this great tract of country, which renders travel in it almost impossible, that has caused its geography to remain obscure. In one of the more recent maps the Everglades are represented as containing splendid rivers, fifty and sixty miles long, diverging from all kinds of imaginary water-sheds. But on careful inspection it will be noticed that some of these rivers have their sources on land, and run up-hill, emptying into no other body of water. In another we notice the Miami River to be thirty miles long, and the Harney River about forty.

Probably as accurate a map as any we have to-day is that issued by the railroad company, and put up in its folders. This is not like the usual railroad publication, which straightens a very crooked road in order to deceive the public into taking what appears the shortest route, but is compiled mostly from the best data in possession of the Interior Department. It may seem strange, in our days of Arctic and African exploration, for the general public to learn that in our very midst, as it were, in one of our Atlantic coast States, we have a tract of land one hundred and thirty miles long and seventy miles wide that is as much unknown to the white man as the heart of Africa. This tract occupies the southern part of the State. It is bounded on the north by Lake Okeechobee, on the east by the pine-land about six miles wide facing the Atlantic, on the south by the mangrove swamps facing the Bay of Florida and the Gulf of Mexico, and on the west by the

Across the Everglades

Big Cypress Swamp which touches the land of the west coast.

Every one has heard of the Everglades; but I think that the general impression of what constitutes the Everglades is absolutely erroneous. If you seek information, you will probably be told that it is a vast tract of swamp in Florida, into which the Indians were driven during the Seminole War, and where "Uncle Sam" was unable to follow them. It will be my endeavor to show, as this account of my last winter's expedition progresses, that the word swamp, as we understand it, has no application whatever to the Everglades; that it is a country of pure water; that this water is moving in one direction or another, depending on the natural topography of the country; that the air is wholesome, pure, and free from disease-germs; that near the coast and the mangroves the mosquitoes thrive; but deep in the Everglades, in the winter time at least, you can sleep comfortably without a net. No stagnant pools exist for the larvæ to thrive in.

The winds blow gently over this almost level expanse most of the time from the southeast, though occasionally they come from the Gulf, and still more rarely sweep down from due

North, when the thermometer drops gradually to about 50°. During the last cold winter, a few years ago, the central and northern part of the State was made desolate, and thousands of people were financially ruined, by the terrible blow given to the orange culture. The northern half of Lake Okeechobee was covered with ice, and the cocoanut-trees were stripped of their leaves at Palm Beach, which is about their northern limit. On Biscayne Bay, however, the cold did no damage. Northers of such low temperature, fortunately, lose most of their cold before reaching South Florida, and the usual daily temperature of the Everglades in the winter is from 70° to 80°. The air has plenty of life in it at all times, and is full of what people call "ozone." Even the heat of 80° seems about the same as 70° in our mid-summer.

Since returning home I have frequently been asked, Did you not suffer from fever ? Were you not made ill by your exposure in that terrible, malarious swamp ? I reply that during the entire winter I did not have a single ache or pain, with the exception of an accident which befell me on the Florida Reefs, in which the bone of my nose was half cut through. This wound, a very bad one, occurred just before I started into the Glades, and healed in a most rapid manner, though exposed to the sun all day. The Indians bear witness to the healthfulness of this region. The men have fine, stalwart figures; the women are strong and in many instances beautiful; the children are fat and chubby. They suffer less from the diseases that Indians are apt to have, and are content in their simple wild life so long as the "lying" white man lets them alone in the one little spot which they have hoped might ever be inaccessible to him.

Over these watery wastes the Seminole still paddles his cypress dug-out canoe, hunts the deer and the otter, and observes the rites and ceremonies of his tribe, unmixed with and uncontaminated by the whites. The occasional visits which he makes to the trading-stations do him no good, as there he finds the " white man's fire-water," which he is tempted to imbibe too freely by those who think themselves of a superior race, but who, in reality, are far inferior to the " untutored Indian" in every moral trait.

The Everglades came into prominence during our war with the Indians, a war of which the United States government has not much to boast. Costing so many lives and so many dollars, it was against a people which was willing to live in peace, but which naturally objected with all its force to the destruction of its homes and the theft of its hogs and cattle. They soon found that redress of their wrongs was impossible, and there was nothing left but to fight, and with such a place of retreat from which to make sorties they certainly did maintain that fight in a marvellous manner. The United States troops, during this war, at various times penetrated the more northerly portions of the Everglades, but, as a rule, the scouting parties were obliged to return, having accomplished little, through their lack of knowledge of the country and for want of food, while the Indians usually followed them back on their trail, knowing their every movement.

One party of soldiers discovered a stronghold of the Seminoles in the Big Cypress Swamp through treachery ; the only instance on record of the Indians being taken by surprise, their knowledge of the country and their method of travel being so much better than that of their enemies. The case to which I refer was recently related to me in a conversation I had with William Mickler, of St. Augustine. A small detach-

ment of Major Loomis's command was on a
scouting expedition a few miles directly south
of Lake Okeechobee. William Mickler climbed
a small tree growing on a wet island, and some
three miles distant saw a very small column of
smoke rising from a little clump of bushes, and
knew that it was an Indian camp-fire.

With the greatest caution the command was
divided, the main body forming the advance ; a
few picked men were given orders to move
around them, and as soon as the advance should
engage to come up and attack the rear. A cover
in the way of small bushes greatly facilitated
the movements of the surrounding party, and
the time was so accurately calculated that at the
first shout of the advance they rushed in, and
the whole band was captured without loss on
either side. The Indians were so unprepared
for this attack that the few guns fired did no
damage. Eighteen men and women were captured, Old Tommy being of the number. This
was quite a bonanza for the soldiers, as previously the whites, exasperated by their want of
success in dealing with these savages, had re-
sorted to many cruelties, giving no quarter.
The government, in order to check this inhuman
warfare, had offered a reward of five hundred

dollars for warriors, three hundred dollars for women, and two hundred dollars for children, if captured alive. Old Tommy was sent to Fort Myers with his fourteen-year-old son, but the lad managed to escape. The imprisonment, and the easy way by which he was trapped, had so wrought upon the old man's feelings that he committed suicide by eating glass.

Many short scouting expeditions were made in the northern part of the Everglades, but when the troops got away from their base of supplies, the travel being slow and uncertain, they experienced terrible hunger and fatigue, and were glad to return to the coast. The Indians, with their knowledge of the country, always travelling rapidly, were not obliged to encumber themselves with many provisions, and easily evaded these parties. At last those who were not captured and sent to the Western Reservation retreated to the far South, and General Worth, finding the absolute impossibility of getting at them, came to a personal understanding that so long as they let the whites alone they should not be disturbed. This compact has been kept by the Indians to the letter, and is as sacred to them to-day as when made. They simply live in fear that the white man will not keep to his part, and that they will be suddenly ordered to the Western Reservation, considering, as they do, that the name " white man" is a synonyme of " liar."

Search well the history of our dealings with this noble race, and judge for yourselves if they are wrong in this definition. I may overestimate their moral characteristics, but this I do know, that a Seminole would as soon cut his tongue out as lie. Whenever an Indian has stated something to be a fact, or has passed his word to me that he would do a certain thing, I have always been able to rely upon what he said to the very letter. When an Indian is found guilty of a malicious lie, his punishment by the council is always a very severe one. Although the Seminoles are to-day perfectly friendly to the whites, and have helped out many a lost white man, who but for timely aid would have starved to death before reaching the coast, nothing will induce them to divulge the secret of Everglade travel, which they alone possess. They may take you out, but never in. Very large sums of money have been offered them to act as guides at different times. One case that I know of was that of an engineer who wished to take his line well into the interior ; but it was of no avail; he was compelled to abandon his project and report to his chief that further carrying of the line was impossible.

The first attempt to make a lengthened journey through any part of the Everglades in the interest of geographical research was made by Major A. P. Williams in 1883, the expense of which was covered by a Southern newspaper. This was called the "Times Democrat Expedition." I regret very much that I have no detailed account of this line, as it must have been very interesting. I fear, however, that accurate surveying must have been abandoned at a very early stage, as I can find no map with any stations, the line being devoid of points from start to finish, and simply gives a general direction from the Harney River to Lake Okeechobee. I can imagine that the fight through the Big Saw Grass, which lies to the south of the lake, must have been a very severe one.

In 1892, Mr. J. E. Ingraham started on an exploring expedition with Mr. J. W. Newman as engineer and twenty men. Some of the details of this trip, taken from his private notes and those of another of his party, I am through his kindness enabled to present to my readers.

On the 15th of March, 1892, the party, consisting of Mr. J. E. Ingraham, Mr. Newman (an engineer), with twenty men, two flat skiffs, and two canvas canoes, started from Fort Myers on the old government trail which leads to Fort Shackelford. The two flat-bottomed skiffs had previously been sent on by ox-cart. The party started with a single horse and wagon, a second team being procured to assist in the carrying. In four days of marching the old government causeway was crossed which passes over the Ocklacoochee Slough and Big Cypress Swamp, which was constructed about 1885. At this juncture a perceptible flow south was noticed in the stream of water comprising a portion of the slough. The prairie which they entered upon after crossing the slough above mentioned extends eastward about forty miles, and is from five to twenty-five miles wide. It is said to be the finest cattle range in the State. A number of different companies had fenced off large pastures, running a fence line from a point in the Big Cypress to the Everglades, a distance of twenty-seven miles. The fence was barbed wire.

Twenty miles was through water from five to six inches deep, at various points the rock appearing on the surface. Where there was rock the soil appeared very poor, being sparsely covered with vegetation. At various points on the stock range the grass was high and thick, and said to be very nutritious and affording wholesome food for cattle, magnificent bodies of cypress timber extending southward along the line of what is known as the Big Cypress. The country appeared to have been cleaned out as far as game was concerned, and it is not surprising that the Indians should have apparently deserted a country so devoid of game. On March 19 an old Indian camp was passed that was occupied by a squaw called Nancy and three grandchildren of about two, four, and five years, two or three dogs, and a lot of chickens. She graciously received the party, and gave them such information as was possible to understand, her stock of English being quite limited. The children were noted for their dignity and reserve, and were fat and healthy. Nancy was asked the distance to Miami, and she replied one hundred miles, and that Indian could go from Shackelford to Miami in four days, and added, with a chuckle, that it would take white man ten days.

Nancy claimed to be the widow of Osceola, a son of the great chief of that name; she is the widow, also, of Billy Jumper, who was drowned in the Miami River a short time ago. One of the hunting-parties found several Indian villages, in which were growing bananas, lemons, and two or three varieties of guavas. Mr. Ingraham received information from a man who accompanied the party, and who claimed to have been there, that the Harney River was forty-four miles long with good water.

On March 21, Fort Shackelford was reached, and one load was sent ahead to the edge of the Everglades, some four miles distance, by means of the ox-team, which was retained for that purpose. The entire party joining, a camp was made a mile and a quarter into the Everglades The surveyors began chaining and levelling from Fort Shackelford, and found a drop of two and three-tenths feet. An Indian named Billy Fiewel was met, and after much persuasion was induced to travel with them, but he very soon left the expedition and was never seen again. The soundings gave from three to five feet of mud overlying the limestone.

An island was passed of about an acre in extent, on which grew wild fig- and rubber-trees. Even in the saw-grass hard rock bottom could always be found with a five-foot pole. Fresh Indian signs were seen ; the Glades here presented an endless sea of saw-grass. The secretary, while engaged in writing, was disturbed by a moccasin snake attempting to crawl up his left shoulder. The only thing in the way of fresh provisions that could be obtained were a few fresh-water turtle, marsh-hens, limpkins, and an occasional mallard duck. On March 25 very heavy saw-grass was encountered, and the fatigue of the men was so great that it was thought best to abandon the smallest of the wooden boats, and some of the impedimenta was thrown away. The level rock here was but twelve inches below the surface. A few small islands were passed, and occasionally one with a little more ground on it.

On March 26 an unfortunate accident occurred to the provisions. The corn meal was packed with bottles of syrup, which fermenting, drove out the corks and was soaked up by the meal; some, however, was used with bread, the flour having been all consumed. The work through the saw-grass was beginning to tell on the men, in the shape of severe pains, cuts, and bruises. When camps were made at night many moccasins were killed. Indian signs were again encountered, their poles sticking up at landing-places on the small islands, and the ground well strewn with the shells of the Ever-glade terrapin which they had eaten. Before starting, in order to arrange about provisions, the average rate of travel had been placed at five miles ; but as this was not realized, it became necessary to reduce the rations. The cook of the party was taken sick and had to be carried in the canoe.

The story of how a nice meal of venison was lost is well told by another member of the party. " As we had not seen any game in the Glades, the guns were usually kept in the boats. This morning, as we were strung out through the saw-grass, I heard, from those in front, shouts of, ' Get the gun ! shoot him ! kill him ! catch him !' and an instant later a deer emerged from the grass in front and plunged heavily in the bog, not twenty yards from me. For an instant the frightened animal seemed stuck in the mud, but gathering himself with all his strength, made a supreme effort and disappeared in the grass just as several of us made a rush to catch him. And when the deer was gone, and there was no prospect of venison steaks for supper, every one of those fellows, who were so tired of hominy, went back to the boats, strapped on their guns, loaded themselves with ammunition, and vowed the next time a deer came they would be ready for him, but I haven't seen a deer since, and I don't think they have either." The travel through the saw-grass became more and more difficult, and packing for any distance seemed impracticable. A few white heron were killed and eaten. A cold northeaster set in, which made a night in wet clothes very uncomfortable. One of the men had managed to boil some rice for supper, but it was only half-done; there was nothing that could be used for fuel excepting the dried saw-grass.

Mr. Newman, the engineer, estimated that it was from twenty-five to twenty-seven miles to Miami. There were but five days' provisions, and it was necessary to put all hands on allowance, their best rate of travel being three miles a day. Surveying became more and more difficult, the chainmen, having so much extra work, on so little to eat, began to give out from physical exhaustion, and for the time that work had to be suspended. For the next day's journey rather better channels were found, the current setting in swifter to the southeast, running about a mile an hour, but as the centre of the Glades was reached the surface became broader and shallower, the water running some-what slower. Seven Everglade terrapin, one marsh-hen, and three fish—the latter jumping into the boats—were caught or shot on this day. During the night two alligators were attracted by the provisions in one of the boats, and had not Mr. Ingraham been sleeping there the party might have been left with nothing to eat. The red bugs were something fearful, and the men were all so peppered over with them that their bodies seemed on fire.

A note was made on the growth of saw-grass, and it was found to be three-quarters of an inch for one night. Camp fifteen was made on a small wet island,. on which were growing custard-apples. Large islands could be seen to the north and east; the water was increasing in depth, in places about two feet; Indian fires were sighted, but no Indians. Food was going rapidly, nothing left but hominy, and the game was scarce. Three blue heron and an alligator were taken, but the alligator was thrown away, as none of the party had the courage to eat it, though they were really in a famished condition by this time.

[As I have frequently eaten alligator when out of food, I think Mr. Ingraham made a great mistake in not trying what effect careful cooking would have had in getting up a very palatable dish. It is, of course, rather difficult to overcome the prejudice most people have against it.—AUTHOR.]

Fish might possibly have been caught, but the time necessary could not be spared on the march, and when camp was reached the men were too exhausted, though there were lines and hooks in the outfit. The engineer, Mr. Newman, estimated the distance to Miami to be nineteen and a half miles. Hard travelling was again encountered, and no place to camp was found but the saw-grass, which was cut, and the water bridged over in the best way possible. The hardships were increased by many of the men, including Mr. Ingraham, being obliged to sleep in wet clothes. The rock below the surface was deeper here than at any point met with, it being from six to six and a half feet. Many statements were made by the men that they saw a high island, or an Indian, ahead, and they began to realize for the first time that the constant looking at the dead level of saw-grass had destroyed their ideas of height.

Wading along almost to the armpits in water,

bushes seemed to be trees, and a few of them clustered together appeared as a forest. Owing to the physical condition of the men, all surveying was abandoned. On April 2 a good open watercourse was found, and many of the men thought that another day at most would see them out of this terrible watery solitude; but they soon discovered their mistake. An object floated by, however, that filled them with hope. It was a very small, insignificant object; in fact, nothing but a piece of paper with a few printed words torn from a flour-sack. To them that water-borne waif spoke volumes; it meant that they were on the Indian trail to Miami. Heavy smoke was sighted to the east, some of the party thinking that it must have been lighted by a relief party coming after them. The narrow watercourses seemed to tend too much to the south, which caused them to make many tedious portages and drags.

The character of the growth was still changing, the brushes getting more plentiful and the saw-grass somewhat less and more resembling prairie. Islands were scarce, but the range of vision was very limited, even by standing as high as possible in the canoe. Some of the deepest mud was here struck; several more things had to be abandoned to lighten the boat, and were cached on a very small island. The men became constantly bogged, and without the help of their comrades would have perished. The rock was about seven feet below the surface, the water in many places being two feet deep. Mr. Ingraham believes that the east side, if reclaimed, contains the largest volume of muck land. A few more fish jumped into the boats, and a few young water-fowl (rather fishy) were procured from their nests. All the men were showing plainly the effects of the hardships they had undergone, their faces being haggard and their eyes bloodshot. Two more of the men gave out entirely, and had to be carried in the boats, more things being thrown away to make room for them. A meal was omitted in order to try and reach an island where wood could be had to cook with and a dry place on which to sleep, if possible.

From the top of a young rubber-tree Mr. Ingraham saw what he took to be pine-timber, about five miles to the eastward, which was very encouraging to every one. At ten P.M. an Indian was seen approaching, who proved to be Billy Harney, a wiry-built man of sixty-five or seventy. An unsuccessful attempt was made to get him to go to Miami with the party, but the most they could get out of him was, that he would get some one else to go, telling them Miami was twenty-five miles away, and pointing in a different direction from what was expected. This intelligence threw the party into the depths of despair, as it would take fully five days to get there, and only enough rations were left on half allowance for two days. Mr. Newman determined to go alone with Billy Harney, and see if he could not procure some provisions and boats and find, if possible, a route to Miami. In the middle of the day, Mr. Newman returned and told the party that he had gone to Harney's camp, but had found nothing but one woman and nothing to eat. The woman told him that he could go to Miami and back in twenty-four hours, if an Indian took him.

He persuaded Billy Harney to accompany him, Mr. Ingraham, and Mr. Moses, Mr. Newman leaving orders to take a certain course the next day and make fires in the saw-grass. The advance party camped on an island at sunset, and the next morning, after a very early start, reached the Miami River, under the Indian's guidance, about nine o'clock. The rapids in the Miami were shot, some of the party walking around through the pine-timber. The drop of the water seemed to be ten feet in three hundred yards. Miami was reached at noon, and the party was warmly welcomed by Mrs. Tuttle, who raised the American flag and fired a salute of dynamite cartridges in their honor. After a good meal and a night of rest from the terrible fatigue, Mr. Newman succeeded in persuading old Matlo and Billy Harney to return to the rescue of the party with provisions. The rescuing party reached the poor sufferers in due time, and every one seemed to get new life at the prospect of reaching the end of their painful journey next day.

After satisfying their hunger, they pushed rapidly on, and camped that night very near the Miami River, where another big meal was indulged in. The next day they joined the advance party at Miami. This finished an expedition that threw much light on what really existed in the way of land between Fort Shackelford and the coast, and the notes from time to time show pretty well the geological formation of the surface rock, the character of the grass, and the islands. The rich lands on which the Indians were supposed to have large, profitable farms and splendid groves of orange-trees and limes certainly did not exist in this section. Were they still in the far south? Perhaps.

CHAPTER II

Preliminary Trip—Seminoles at Home—Details of Outfit.

IT was after a conversation with Mr. Ingraham that I became interested in the southern part of the Everglades, which had as yet been unexplored. I then became possessed with the idea that I must go and find out for myself some of the mysteries of this *terra incognita*. From my early experiences in canoeing in the Adirondacks, the Maine woods, and Canada, I thought I could turn my back on my base of supplies, and with an exceedingly small party, a well thought-over and weight-calculated outfit, manage to live without unendurable privation for at least two months, if necessary, even if the country would not support me. I fear I seemed a little boastful to Mr. Ingraham in saying that I intended to make the attempt to cross the Everglades without sleeping in wet clothes, for I never remembered having done so in all my out-door life. Let it be set down to my credit that I did not say that I would, but that I would try to do it. I am glad to say now that my trip is ended, that I have been successful, especially about the wet clothes, as I never have been troubled with rheumatism, and if I had not succeeded on this point, I am afraid I would not now be writing so comfortably in my little den at home.

In making my proposed trip there were three things that I had in mind: First, the geographical exploration of the southern part of the Everglades and the making of an accurate line, the stations of which I intended to verify with my sextant, as has been my wont to do at sea. Secondly, the surveying of a channel through the Ten Thousand Islands and a reconnoissance of the southwest coast, for the confidential charts of the United States Naval War College (in which I had taken a two years' course). Thirdly, the collection of specimens of natural history for the University of Pennsylvania.

In order to be well posted for such an expedition, I thoroughly familiarized myself with the method the Indians adopt in travelling (for they alone have the secret). I started in the winter of 1896, after procuring an Indian canoe, one of the medium size (they vary in length from fourteen to thirty feet), with a hunter by

the name of Ed. Brewer, whom I had accidentally met. This man had been among the Indians for many years, in his hunting trips, and
had the natural faculty of the backwoodsman
in following a trail; moreover, he was a splendid poler. The skilful use of the pole is an
absolute necessity in work in the Everglades.
The Seminole hardly knows the use of the
paddle; even on salt water he poles or sails
round the coast. In the Everglades the paddle
is useless, and if you break a pole and have not
a second one with you, you are in very bad
plight indeed, as straight saplings are hard to
find. The poles used are procured mostly from
near the coast. On these poles, about one inch
from the lower and larger end, a triangular inverted bracket, or foot, is nailed, like that put
on the stilts of our childhood. The portion
of the pole that projects beyond the bracket
prevents slipping on the rock, and its lower
surface, together with that of the inverted
bracket, stops the pole from sinking very far
into the mud. The Indians use this pole with
a skill that can only come of practice from
infancy. The canoes are hollowed from a
cypress-log, and are quite narrow for their
length, rather sharp on the water-line forward,

but above-water flaring out suddenly into a blunt bow, well narrowed at the stern, and finishing in an overhang.

Though the cypress-wood is rather light, the bottom and sides are so thick that they will weigh two or three hundred pounds. A seat is formed in the stern partly upon the overhang, and the surface helped out by a few boards. On this seat, which is pretty high, the poler stands, giving, besides the push, a very good guiding force. The extra elevation helps him very much in seeing over the tall grass, and judging which water leads are the best to follow. It is astonishing how much the bows of these canoes resemble some made by the Alaska Indians. Formerly many painted their canoes white and indulged in much ornamentation about the bows in red paint, with the boat's name in letters on the side. The universal color now seems to be black, with little or no ornamentation. In a canoe such as I have described (built by Tiger Tail thirty years ago, and used by various Indians previous to coming into my possession) my wife, my eleven-year-old son, Ed. Brewer, and myself started on our expedition, leaving our little yacht at the mouth of the swift stream.

Across the Everglades

The sun was just rising, and a pleasant, cool breeze ruffled the surface of the river. Brewer with his pole in the stern, and myself with the Canadian paddle in the bow, made rapid headway against the current, which was getting stronger and stronger. The river winds in beautiful curves, the trees growing to the water's edge, and were it not for the occasional cocoanut-tree or cabbage-palm, you would almost imagine yourself in one of the wild streams of the Maine woods. Very soon we saw large white objects ahead, which proved to be balls of foam hurrying down with the current. With a quick turn to the left, after about three miles of paddling, we struck the South Fork, the water becoming swifter and swifter, and the cotton-like balls larger and more numerous. We were on the falls, and how the water did run! I could hear Brewer panting behind me, but I never turned my head or gave any signal that we were conquered, but started in on my old-time stroke, inch by inch crawling up that water, dodging the rocks. After about three-quarters of an hour of the hardest paddling I think I have ever done, the water slowed up a little, and we could get some speed on the canoe. The trees opened up

more, the stream becoming narrower and narrower, until we came to an opening where
everything was clear ahead.

This was the edge of the Everglades, and the
place for which the Indians make when bound
to the coast by way of the Miami River. The
stream here loses itself among the lily-pads and
before you lies a sea of apparently pathless
grass. On closer observation shallow watercourses are seen running through the grass,
cutting in all directions, spreading out like the
lines in the human hand, and whichever one
you take you regret that you did not choose
the other.

Brewer knew the general direction of the
camp, as he had previously visited it, and,
though headed off several times, did not go
very much off his course. It was along this
Indian trail that I noticed for the first time
an enormous quantity of a certain kind of
plant, called by naturalists *Cabomba Caroliniana*,
growing in very large patches. There must
have been tons of it. Surely this plant must
be a great factor in keeping the water so
clear, as it is the same sold by goldfish dealers
in our cities to put in self-sustaining aquaria,
at ten cents a bunch. Much of this we poled

through, and other grasses, of which I will speak later. For five miles we pushed out into the Glades, and reached one of the large islands we had seen from a distance. Rounding a turn of the island, we came upon a rude landing made of wreckage from the coast, with light timbers and planks. The Indians transport these very long distances, lashed to their canoes on the outside. Numerous poles were stuck at random, where they were left by their owners.

Close to this wharf were a number of canoes of different sizes, and standing in one of the largest was an Indian working, and doing very hard work, too. He did not appear to be ashamed of it, which surprised me greatly. Fancy an Apache doing even the most trivial thing to relieve the squaws from their arduous camp duties! In front of this Indian (who proved to be Miami Jimmy) was a very curious piece of mechanism. It was a sheet of tin roofing about three feet square, in which holes about half an inch apart had been driven, with the rough side up, and he was using it like a nutmeg-grater. The Indian was rubbing very violently back and forth the roots of the coonti plant. The starch made from this plant is a staple article of food with them. It tastes a little like arrowroot and is exceedingly nutritious and healthy. Growing in great abundance on the pine-land, it is also gathered by the whites and converted into starch by a more elaborate process than that used by the Indians.

As we passed on towards the centre of the island, we saw a few braves standing about, the remainder of the men being out on a hunt, but not a woman or child anywhere in sight. All had run away to hide behind trees or under the shelter of their palmetto shacks. These shacks, or huts, are framed with four upright pieces, a floor, made of drift-wood, being placed about three feet from the ground, on which are strewn deer-skins. This structure is covered overhead by a thatching of palmetto-leaves. The sides are usually open, but at night curtains made of canvas or bagging are dropped on two sides to protect against the wind and rain.

It was only when they found that we intended no harm that they came out, eying us curiously and distrustfully, the sight of a white woman in the Everglades being of most unusual occurrence. About eight men, six squaws, and ten pickaninnies composed the camp. The squaws were dressed in a very tasteful, modest manner; their skirts, about to their ankles, were made of blue or brown calico, and trimmed with bright red or yellow bands, stitched in odd designs; little zouave jackets with long sleeves, made of some bright-colored calico, which did not meet the skirt belt by several inches, leaving their bronze skin exposed, completed the costume. But their chief and most prized ornaments are strings of colored beads. They are very particular about the kind of bead. It must be solid and about the size of a small pea, they being especially fond of turquoise blue and light red. One woman had over twenty-five pounds of these around her neck. As they are worn all the time it must be rather a heavy burden to carry. The children were exceedingly bright and disposed to be friendly with the small boy of our party. One of Little Tiger's sons sold a small canoe that he had made himself, and a bow and arrows. The bow was about four feet long, rather flat in shape. The arrows were tipped with empty pistol cartridges, old spools, and bits of iron. We had a quantity of beads with us, and were able to bargain with them for some " sofke" spoons, which is their one article of table service, each one dipping it into the cooking-pot in turn. It is a carved wooden spoon about the size of a soup-ladle. Bead-work articles, buckskin leggings, tanned deer-skins, and otter-hides were scattered about the camp. All seemed to be doing something, and went on with their work, not paying the slightest attention to us.

Two Indians were skinning some freshly killed otters on a wooden platform. In one corner a squaw had a great prize in the shape of a rusty, hand sewing-machine, which was no doubt the envy of the rest of the women. She was working with great diligence, squatting on the ground in front of it. This industry was frequently interrupted by the snapping of the thread, which seemed to bother her a great deal; no doubt she had many misgivings as to whether it would not be more profitable to return to her more primitive method.

The dandy of the camp, " Willie Tiger," whose Indian name is " Coacochee," spoke a little English. I had made his acquaintance the week before on the shores of Biscayne Bay, and had told him that in seven days I would meet him at his camp in the Everglades. He replied, with a very doubtful expression on his face, " You white man no lie?" and when he saw us, if an Indian could look surprised, he certainly did. Dr. Tiger was very gorgeous in his deer-skin leggings, moccasins, white shirt, and red turban, which head-dress is a characteristic of the Seminole's attire, being made of a shawl twisted round and knotted. This turban has several other purposes besides mere ornament. At night it is sometimes unwound and used as a covering. The bright colors in it are of much value in attracting the attention of a deer, and it is frequently used for this purpose while hunting. The rest of the men were barelegged and bareheaded, with a calico shirt belted around the waist. Their hair was cut short, with the exception of a straight bang. The women wore their hair drawn into a knot, and also wore the bang. Silver ear-rings are worn by men, women, and children. Formerly there was much more hammered silver used than at present, as the Indians have become poorer and poorer; many of the large silver crescents having long ago found their way to the trading-post.

At different times they have had among them men who were quite noted as silver-smiths and became celebrated throughout the tribe. The squaws make very pretty bead-work belts, bags, and ornaments. They also make neat baskets, which they use for all conceivable purposes.

After leaving the camp we retraced our steps to the landing, where we found "Miami Jimmy" still working at his huge nutmeg-grater. I had left my canoe close to where he was at work, and, although there were many things in sight which must have been interesting to him, nothing had been disturbed. As a rule, you may place implicit confidence in the honesty of a Seminole. Before leaving I showed him the mechanism of my three-barrelled gun, which he seemed to understand perfectly, and thought "heap good."

Loading the canoe, we took our homeward course, following very nearly the one on which we had come, reaching the source of the Miami late in the afternoon by hard and rapid poling. The travel down stream was very swift, and when the falls were reached the canoe was moving like a torpedo-boat. It seemed hardly any time before Biscayne Bay was sighted, just as the sun was making one of those gloriously colored skies which are only seen in Southern Florida.

I had learned much on this little trip that I hoped would be useful to me, as I had now fully determined during the next winter to cross the Everglades and make careful note of everything that I should see, and if possible to plot my course in such a way that it might be of some scientific value to geographical and zoological research. With this idea I searched all the maps, ancient and modern, and read all the books on Florida that I could find.

Having spent three months, for the past twenty winters, in hunting, fishing, canoeing, and yachting around the coast, I was in very good training to undertake this journey. During the summer of 1896 I began my preparations, and as an old sportsman made long lists from which to make up my outfit, which were eventually to be cut down to attain the minimum weight. The first thing to occupy my attention was what kind of boat I should use. My old shadow cruising canoe was out of the question in a place where the pole had to be used so constantly, and she would not carry enough for so long a journey with such slender chance of replenishing provisions; moreover, the standing position is imperative, in order to look over the tall grass and find your road. A sail I thought might be of use, but eventually I abandoned that. My first thought was a Seminole dug-out, but thinking that I might have to make some long portages, I decided that a lighter canoe would be more serviceable. I entered into correspondence with one of our best canoe-builders, who had been my personal friend in the early days of the American Canoe Association, and gave him an order to build me two canoes. Having spent so much time in the Maine woods, and frequently noted over what shoal water the Canadian model could travel with a good load, and that the light frame and planking, covered with canvas, could be readily mended in case of accident, I accordingly gave my order for this model, the first canoe to be sixteen feet long and thirty inches beam, to be called " Coacochee ;" the second fourteen feet long and thirty inches beam, to be called " Hissee." One of these boats, the " Hissee," was sent to my home in Newport, that I might experiment with her and add all those little extra arrangements so dear to the heart of a canoeist. The " Coacochee" was sent direct to St. Augustine, where the " Hissee" joined her a little later. A single sail was given each canoe (the Bailey rig), with forty square feet in each.

The getting together of a camp outfit is always interesting, and the peculiarity of the place in which it was to be used made it doubly so. There are certain standard things that I have used for many years, and always keep in a trunk, that I bring out when contemplating a trip to the woods. Sleeping-bags I take whether I go to a cold or a hot climate. They are simply made of two heavy blankets. The first blanket is sewed up into a long bag, with a good slit in the top of it ; the second is sewed in the same manner, but with a muslin cover. The second covering serves to keep the bags clean, and adds to their warmth by stopping some of the air from passing through. On a warm night the single, uncovered bag is used, and on a cold one the second is added.

A rubber bed was purchased as an experiment, but the experiment was a failure, and ended by my sleeping on it without blowing it up, as whenever I would turn over it would roar like an alligator, and it bulged so in the middle that I would constantly roll off. A rubber ground sheet was of course indispensable. For a pillow I used my coat, which I found better than rubber pillows. A full suit of rubber mackintosh made by a Boston firm, in the same shape as " oil-skins," which keep you dry all day in a pouring rain, I always kept loose in

the canoe, this being the only extra outer clothing carried. The suit I habitually wear consist-
of a brown tweed Norfolk jacket with knicker-
bockers, brown flannel shirt, leather leggings to
protect as much as possible from snakes and
mosquitoes, and heavy leather shoes, with tennis
shoes to wear in the canoe, which slip off easily
when preparing for wading, when rubber hip
boots are put on. These I consider absolutely
indispensable for a white man travelling in the
Everglades.

The clothing and sundry list included an
extra pair of long woollen stockings, one pair
of drawers, five handkerchiefs, one undershirt,
and one brown flannel shirt. The sleeping-bags
and clothing go into a rubber mackintosh bag
in the daytime; the rubber ground sheet is left
out to cover things in the canoe in case of a
shower. In a game-bag is carried soap (in
aluminum box), letter paper, note-books, spy-
glass, linen rags, rubber surgical plaster, comb,
tobacco, tooth-brush, tooth-powder in tube,
small medicine-case containing cholera mixture,
castor oil, quinine pills, aristol, carbolized sinew
(for sewing wounds), zinc ointment, and colo-
cynth pills; a pocket surgical case containing
many necessary instruments in a small compass,

also a clinical thermometer, a small bag with scissors, needles, thread, and buttons, pocket-compass, small whiskey-flask, veil for hat, with two elastic bands, one fitting round the neck the other round the top of the hat, two lead-pencils, small fishing-bag containing one heavy trolling line, one light trolling line float, sinkers, hooks, one large spoon, one small spoon, and six red ibis flies.

My scientific instrument case, which could be dispensed with on an ordinary hunting trip, contained an octant, an aluminum aneroid barometer, a maximum and minimum register-ing thermometer mounted on aluminum, an ar-tificial horizon, a lock level, a light but very ac-curate azimuth compass with four-inch dial, and two watches in a waterproof case, the watches themselves being waterproof, running with an accuracy that was something marvellous, one having a rate of four-tenths of a second a day, and the other eight-tenths of a second. These watches were supplied to me by a chronometer-maker of Philadelphia, who had been regu-lating them on Greenwich time for many months.

The artificial horizon was not the one of mercury which I have generally carried when using a sextant on shore, but was a black mirror. I am aware that the use of a mirror is not orthodox, and that all the old books on navigation say that a mirror cannot be used on account of the refraction in the glass, which error is so variable that it cannot be properly tabulated, but being determined to do away with the weight that mercury would involve, and its liability to spill, I made a visit in my perplexity to my old professor in physics, at the University of Pennsylvania, and when I suggested " mirror," he said to me, " I have just the thing you want ; come into the physical laboratory. Here is a black mirror whose anterior surface alone gives the true reflection. I use it in astronomical work and the measurement of light waves." It was mounted on three posts, with slow motion thumb-screws, so that it could be levelled with a small spirit level with quickness and accuracy. The mirror was backed with brass in such a way that it would be difficult to break, and a protective pad was always kept on its surface when packed for travelling. This was a find for me, as I had no doubt that I could use it in taking meridian altitudes, and long and careful experiment in comparison with mercury proved that I was correct.

Across the Everglades

One of the most important things in a life out of doors is the selection of a tent. A perfect tent should cover the maximum ground with the minimum weight of muslin, and should have but one pole. Choosing from a geometric figure, the cone tent seems to fill these requirements, and for many years I have used such a tent, adding a small awning to shelter the sloping door from the rain. I thought this was as near perfection as could be obtained, until at the World's Fair at Chicago I spied, in a corner of the Fisheries Exhibit, a tent the merits of which could not be disputed ; it could be used in so many different ways to suit the nature of the ground. It had but one pole, the door was vertical, there was a wall where a wall was required, with the greatest head-room near the door. A fly was used that could be arranged in many different ways, as protection from extra heavy rains, or placed in front, nearly doubling the available room and ground covered. This tent I added to the outfit, with its jointed pole, all stowing nicely in a canvas bag with shoulder straps and weighing complete twenty pounds. Many a time in the Everglades I pitched a part of this tent, and made a comfortable shelter for the night, where no other tent would have been of the slightest use.

During the summer evenings I made of very light wood two chests that formed convenient packages to load and unload from a canoe, the dimensions being twenty-two inches by thirteen, and nine inches in depth. These chests made very good seats or tables. The first, which I called my cooking chest, was divided by a bulkhead running across the box. In the left compartment was the aluminum cooking outfit, which weighed six pounds. It consisted of an outer cooking-pot, a second nearly the same size nesting into it; inside of this was a frying-pan and three plates; on the plates rested a coffee-pot; in the coffee-pot were three cups (nested), pepper and salt, three knives, three spoons, and three forks. The pots and frying-pan had detachable handles. The right-hand compartment contained bacon, portable foods of various kinds in pots and cans, also fresh provisions.

I had three varieties of portable soups; tea, root-beer, lemonade, and sarsaparilla put up in tablets, and condensed cola-nut preparations; also a good supply of chewing-gum (containing cola-nut). The second chest I called the grocery chest. It contained large-mouthed, screw-top cans of various sizes, closing water-tight, with rubber gaskets; these were marked sugar, flour, salt, pepper, oatmeal, cocoa-leaves, cocoa, paint and varnish for canoes, and a sealed can of whiskey exclusively for snake-bite. In this way I had no fear of anything getting wet or spoiling. The canoe might upset, and I could go ashore, cook my supper, and sleep in dry clothes.

The kerosene-stove and a lantern were carried loose in the boat. The stove was an experiment, but proved a great success, as I had many a hot meal in places where no fire could be made, and the flame burns well in the open air. I have cooked over naphtha-stoves for many years at sea without accident, but have never felt safe in leaving them in the hands of careless stewards, for if one burner goes out, it converts the galley into a first-rate dynamite cartridge, which the lighted one touches off, and there you are! Of kerosene-stoves I have tried many, as they came out; those with wicks were discarded at once; some burning kerosene vapor were used for a while, but one and all smutted the pots and blew out easily, besides using too much fuel. The stove that I decided to take with me seemed to combine all the virtues that a properly behaved stove should have ; its trade-name I will suppress, as I do not intend to lend these pages to any kind of adver· tisements, though the temptation is great to recommend a really good thing. In the way of hunting and defensive implements I carried a repeating rifle shooting a 45-90 cartridge with steel-covered bullet. Last year I had such poor success, losing many crocodile on which I had made good shots with a 38-55, and rumors coming to me that I should probably meet with a stray puma or a large gray wolf, that I made up my mind I would carry something that would be more successful. A three-barrelled gun (carried by my hunter), two barrels, 16-gauge shot, with rifle barrel underneath of 38-55 calibre. A long 38-calibre revolver and a six-inch hunting-knife completed the equipment, with a box containing fifteen pounds of cartridges.

One thing that greatly troubled me was how to obtain my distance travelled with any accuracy. Chaining was proved by the two former expeditions to be out of the question, and it certainly was necessary to have something to work up the dead reckoning by, and know as nearly as possible the distance covered by the canoe. I had often used my bicycle to measure the miles between the house and the post-office, or the number of yards across a patch of lawn, and found that the cyclometer would measure within ten yards very accurately, so why could not some arrangement of the wheel be used on water and through the grass? No arrangement of any kind of log used at sea would be practicable, so I obtained an old twenty-eight-inch front wheel and a front fork which came from a thirty-inch bicycle; to this I added a new cyclometer and pneumatic tire, and a band of paddles that buckled on the de-inflated tire, which by using the air-pump made a very rigid paddle-wheel. I then fitted a stick that lashed to either side of the canoe, keeping the wheel in a vertical position. After repeated experiments with this machine I found that the slip was very constant, and that trailing behind a boat I could get good measurement, at even a slow rate of speed.

After completing all the little details of this outfit, I shipped canoes and boxes to Miami, in order to have everything well in advance of me, and left my home for Philadelphia, where I spent a month in study at the Natural History

Across the Everglades

Museums and the University of Pennsylvania, taking many meridian altitudes, brushing up my navigation, and trying to work under the conditions that I imagined would confront me. It was my desire to inform myself of the fauna and flora of the State of Florida, in order to allow nothing that was strange or peculiar in animal or flower to escape me, and to be able to collect intelligently any prehistoric relics that might come in my way.

On the 10th day of December I left Philadelphia, alone, leaving my wife and family with friends, and started by rail for St. Augustine, where I arrived on the afternoon of the next day. Here I tarried a week among my old friends, and then proceeded to Miami. Through the courtesy of the railroad company all my things had been sent down to their warehouse on the Miami River dock, which had just been completed. Everything had arrived and was uninjured in transportation, much to my relief. My next move was to communicate with Ed. Brewer, who had hunted with me the year before, and tell him to come at once to Miami and prepare himself for a big trip across the Everglades.

CHAPTER III

Miami—Fowey Rocks Light-House—Florida Wreckers
—Vaseline à la Seminole—Soldier Key—The Habitat
of the Crocodilus Americanus—The North American
Alligator.

MY original idea was to start from either
the head of the Miami River or the
head of New River and take a general
westerly course, which would carry me through
the very centre of the unexplored and unknown
portion. On mature deliberation I gave up this
route, and decided to enter from the west coast,
in the vicinity of the Ten Thousand Islands
archipelago, and come out on the Atlantic.

The reason for my change of direction was
this : Going west, I would come out upon an
entirely uninhabited coast ; the distance from
the edge of the Glades to the Gulf of Mexico
is great, and after leaving the fresh water I
would not be able to carry a sufficient quantity
in the canoes to reach any spot where I could
procure more, and it would be impossible for
me to indicate a definite place where a boat

could meet me. On the other hand, going first around to the Gulf with a good load of supplies and fresh water after making the journey across, I would carry the fresh water to within a very few miles of the Everglades, and on the other side be sure to strike Mr. Flagler's new railroad, which was just completed to Miami.

Deciding on this latter plan, the first requisite was to procure a boat of suitable size in which to proceed around the coast with my two canoes, my entire outfit, and about one hundred gallons of water. After looking over many boats at Miami, I could find nothing that suited me, many of them being unnecessarily large and drawing too much water. I wished nothing that drew over two feet. At last I was told of a boat that was on the ways at Cocoanut Grove, which if I liked and put in order I could get on reasonable terms. I made a trip to Cocoanut Grove and found a very good sloop, thirty feet long, good beam, and drawing two feet, called the " Cupid." She had been built by Ivanosky, of St. Augustine, and was of the type that does such good service around that city, being fast, and carrying a heavy load on light draft.

Across the Everglades

Finding that it would take me a week to put her in commission, I returned to Miami for my trunk, and moved over immediately to the hospitable shelter of the Peacock Inn at Cocoanut Grove. With the assistance of a Bahama darky, I put the little ship in seaworthy condition, and at the end of the week began to look around for a good man who would be sufficiently familiar with the coast to bring the "Cupid" back again after leaving Brewer and myself to start our journey into the mysterious Everglades. Such a man I found in the person of Sam Roberts. Sam was a man of medium stature, powerfully built, and of a pleasant disposition; he was a native of the Bahama Islands, and, like most of his countrymen, was a good sailor, swimmer, and diver. He had spent a great deal of his time in sponge-fishing, and was quite an adept in the business, had been on several excursions around the west coast, and was quite familiar with the Florida Keys.

As soon as the "Cupid" was ready, Sam joined me, and after filling our water-casks at the beautiful, bubbling spring belonging to my old friend, Mr. Kirk Munroe, and bidding adieu to my many acquaintances at the Peacock Inn

and the Biscayne Bay Yacht Club, I sailed for
Miami. That evening Ed. Brewer reported
to me at the railroad warehouse, on the river
front. I gave him orders to procure three Indian poles, and to join me at the railroad warehouse, and we would load the " Cupid" for her
voyage. What a change had been made in this
place since the same time last year !—from two
houses it has been made a town of two thousand
inhabitants. Of course, its splendid big hotel,
with every modern convenience, will prove a
great boon to the tourist, but for me the pict-
uresqueness seemed to have gone ; its wildness
has been rudely marred by the hand of civilization.

In all Florida I have never seen a more
beautiful spot than where this deep, narrow
river suddenly opens into Biscayne Bay between those tall, graceful cocoanut-trees, that
seem to stand as sentinels guarding the secrets
of its source, the mysterious Everglades. Of
course, it will all be very beautiful around the
hotel when the tropical vegetation will have
grown up, as a large sum of money has been
spent, and no doubt the majority will prefer it
as they see it to-day, but, as far as I am concerned, I regret the change. All who have

seen the enormous increase of hotels in the Adirondacks will appreciate this feeling. But in the nature of things the wilderness must be gradually encroached upon. What would the settler and the farmer do without this railroad that now gives him rapid communication with the North for his winter products?

We must not look upon these things from the sentimental point of view. The romance and poetry must be suppressed for the sterner, material welfare of our fellow-man. Early next morning Ed. Brewer came on board with the poles. I got the " Cupid" under way with easy canvas and ran up the river to the freight-house to receive my load. Ed. Brewer was a Virginian by birth, but had lived in Florida for many years, and had always made a living by hunting and trapping. He would sometimes be in the woods, and partly in the Everglades, for six months at a stretch, without seeing a soul except an occasional Indian. He was a man of medium height, heavily built without being fat, black hair, black eyes, inured to hardship, and able to make himself comfortable in his long tramps, with a canoe, a tin pot, a blanket, a deer-skin, a mosquito-bar, and a rifle, with perhaps a plug or two of tobacco as a luxury.

Across the Everglades

My experience in hunting with him the year previous had shown that he was just the man to face with me whatever dangers there might be in store in my attempt to cross the Everglades. Although warned by some of my friends that he was a dangerous character, I preferred to rely upon my own judgment of human nature rather than on unproved stories about him. In our solitary companionship, far from the reach of any law but that of our own making, I always found him brave and industrious, constantly denying himself, deceiving me as to his appetite when our supplies ran low that I might be the more comfortable, and many a night did he stay up an extra hour, while I was finishing my notes and plotting work, that he might tuck me in my cheese cloth from the outside. A few hundred yards up the river brought us to the strongly built dock belonging to the railroad company, and on it rests an object which has an unusual interest, as it is the most southerly piece of railroad iron in the United States.

The work of breaking up boxes and transferring things to the "Cupid" occupied most of the morning. On the 29th of December we started from Miami and ran to Cocoanut

Grove, the wind being light, and stopped there to pick up some things that we wanted and could not get at Miami. The next morning at nine o'clock we sailed for the South. The canoes were lashed partly under the " summer cabin" when under way, and when at anchor were put overboard in order to make plenty of room.

All along this shore there are places where the fresh water comes up through the rock under the salt water with quite a head. It no doubt comes from the Everglades by subterranean passages. The shoal water here reaches quite a distance from shore. The weather had been threatening, and large masses of clouds were being driven by; occasionally one of these would drop its moisture in the shape of a tropical shower, that wets you to the skin before you can put on a rubber coat.

At about eleven o'clock we were abreast an island inshore, near a little settlement called Cutler. It is situated on the Perrine Grant, which has been under litigation for many years, and has the most southerly post-office on the main land of the United States. The building itself is a very unique affair, and is a puzzle that the visitor is curious to solve. The weighty mail matter is handled by the pretty postmistress in the body of an old freight-car. How did that freight-car get to its present resting-place? The more you look at it the more you wonder. The railroad has but just reached Miami, and this is fifteen miles away. When I visited the place later in the year, I asked the postmistress where she obtained her peculiar dwelling, and she told me that a few years ago a steamer loaded with the running equipment of a railroad had been wrecked on the beach beyond the bay, and that the box of a freight-car was floated to Cutler.

The rain-squalls continued, greatly to our annoyance, but we were fast losing sight of the Fowey Rocks Light-House. This light is the first of the light-houses on the Hawk Channel, and marks the entrance of that peculiar inside passage which before the days of light-houses was such a haunt for the pirate and the wrecker. There are several of these lights that mark the outer reef. This particular one was built in 1886. The French lens was on exhibition at Philadelphia and immediately brought South to complete the structure. It now shines forth to the Gulf Stream bewildered mariner at a height of one hundred and ten feet above the level of the Atlantic. Around this light-house seems to be a favorite haunt of fish; perhaps they are attracted there at night and are too lazy to move off in the daytime. Their number and variety are simply marvellous. You can at one glance, through this crystal water, see over fifty varieties. The colors would put to blush the palette of an " impressionist."

The nearest land to the " Light" is a little island called Soldier Key, which was used by the constructing engineers to work upon and for a supply station. The old buildings are still to be seen, though they have never had any attention or care since. Biscayne Bay now began to narrow up, and passing Elliot's Key we see a lot of small islands to our left, where lies Cæsar's Creek, named after a famous old pirate called Black Cæsar. Countless are the interesting and romantic tales told about him and the days when " gentlemen" of his profession added one more risk to marine insurance.

All the surroundings here seem to be filled with legends; you meet constantly something that reminds you of the old days of the " Florida wreckers." On many of the small islands quite large sums of money have been unearthed at different times. This whole stretch of coast has been for centuries a ship's graveyard. Even at the present time tombstones in the shape of a rudder-post, two or three fractured ribs, or the section of a keelson, are constantly visible, and hardly a month passes but some lumber-laden vessel loses, at least, her deck load.

Speaking of wrecks, a rather funny incident occurred a few years ago. A large steamer was stranded on the reef not far from Cape Florida ; no sooner had she struck than the news spread rapidly along the shore, and within an incredibly short space of time the people for twenty miles around gathered on the beach opposite the scene of disaster. Two or three families of Indians chanced to be down from the Everglades, and they too, being keen wreckers, started at once for the beach.

The ship was loaded with quite a valuable assorted cargo, and as she began to break up the ocean was strewn with barrels, cases, and boxes of all kinds. These drifted gradually ashore,—casks of wine, bags of flour, boxes of Colgate's soap, a carriage (which is in use to-day at Cocoanut Grove), and a thousand and one different articles. The Indians soon possessed themselves of a box containing bottles of wine of iron, and it was not very long before they were in a condition that allowed the white men to secure the larger prizes.

The squaws had struck a bonanza in the shape of a case containing Cheeseborough's vaseline, which they mistook for some variety of the white man's cooking-fat. After starting a fire, they proceeded very leisurely to fry their pancakes in it. What a dish for the stomach of an epicurean,—pancakes fried in vaseline *à la* Seminole!

Continuing our course to the southward, we soon reached the narrow channel abreast Arseniker Keys, in which there is but three feet of water at times, and only two stakes to mark it; these are often knocked down by boats from Key Largo. We emerged into Card Sound, which is six miles long by three and a half wide,—a fine sheet of water with good depth. We were now approaching a place that I was anxious to visit, as being one of the few localities where crocodile could be found. I had promised to obtain some good specimens, if possible, for the University of Pennsylvania and the Academy of Natural Science. I therefore decided to spend two days in hunting. It has been known but a short time that the crocodile exists in North America. Usually, when you speak about them, you are told, " I suppose you mean alligators."

Early in the morning, Brewer and myself started in the " Hissee" with our guns to make a thorough reconnoissance of the shore and run up any small creeks that we might find, in search of these formidable and interesting creatures. I say formidable, for in this, as in many other respects, they differ from the alligator. My hunting of the year previous, when I had killed three, had given me somewhat of an insight into their habits; but there were certain facts in regard to them that from a scientific point of view I was anxious to solve. We had just rounded a point of land, and were still moving very slowly, when my eye caught an object on a point about half a mile off that from the distance seemed to be the trunk of a tree, and it was only when I got much nearer that I discovered it to be a crocodile larger than any one I had ever seen before.

Several times I had observed that their color was of an ashen gray, but this one was as light as an old sun-dried stump, a great contrast to the glossy black of the alligator. I soon saw that this old fellow was anything but asleep, but the difficulty was to get near enough to make a sure shot, for if your bullet does not enter the spinal column, you might just as well use quail shot. My favorite shot is to sever the spine just in front of the fore-shoulder. Unfortunately, as he was to leeward of my position, there was no way for me to get the wind of him, although I paddled without noise or splash. He began to move gently, straightening himself up half-way on his legs, which gave me a chance to see his full length. I am almost afraid to state what I consider that length to have been, but as I sent two specimens North later in the winter, one of which measured thirteen feet, and I had killed several the winter before, my estimate of his length must have been quite accurate.

With a gentle slide, and without splash, this splendid fellow sank and was seen no more. Every inch of that beach and of his huge crawl is photographed on my memory. I have vowed that next winter, if his capture is possible, he may yet adorn the walls of some natural history museum. After an unsuccessful attempt to get a shot at a smaller crocodile, Brewer and I returned to the "Cupid" for supper. The earliest account I have been able to get from natives of the State of the occurrence of crocodile was in 1877. By a curious condition of wind and weather the water of the ocean had encroached upon the land, backing up the St. John's River and the easterly bound streams of Southern Florida. Not far from the edge of Lake Okeechobee some Indians who belonged to the tribe that lived in the vicinity of the Kissimmee River captured a crocodile and took it to Kissimmee, where it was recognized by the whites as being a distinct variety from the alligator, with which they were so familiar.

The Indians have probably known of its existence from the earliest times, and in their language called it the " sharp-nosed alligator." The habitat of the *Crocodilus Americanus* is rather difficult to define, but I think that in very early times it could have been found in detached families along the whole sea-coast of the State. Its propagation is much less rapid than the alligator ; they never affiliate, being bitter foes. The fights that occur between them are very unequal conflicts. The broad snout, short teeth, and less active body of the alligator are no match for the narrow jaw, long sharp teeth, and greater ferocity of the crocodile.

Across the Everglades

On one of my hunting expeditions I was fortunate enough to find the nest of this reptile, and employed my hunter to obtain the eggs during the succeeding summer. The eggs were given to the Smithsonian and other museums, and were the first that have ever been presented. I was much struck by the difference of this nest and that made by the alligator, who deposits its eggs well back from the fresh-water stream on which he lives, hidden in vegetation, with a mound erected over the hole consisting of leaves, stumps, broken pieces of wood, and vegetable mould, about two feet high and four feet in diameter; in this the female deposits from one hundred to three hundred eggs.

The crocodile, on the other hand, makes its nest on the edge of the salt water, in a very similar manner to that of the green turtle. A hole is scooped out of the dry sand low enough to insure the proper amount of moisture (independent of rains), which is so important for incubation. The eggs are then laid in layers and the sand smoothed down perfectly level, which makes the place very difficult to find. As I have had but two nests under my observation, it would be rather rash for me to generalize as to the number of eggs the crocodile deposits, but I am under the impression that it is far less than that laid by the alligator. The nests referred to contained, respectively, fifty and seventy-five eggs. I have not been able to prove that the female crocodile returns to the nest at the time of hatching, as is stated of the alligator, but the presumption is that she does. I attempted to hatch eggs last summer, but not being aware of the amount of moisture necessary, succeeded only in drying them up.

My hunter in South Florida was more successful in hatching three, which, however, died afterwards. These specimens, I believe, are the only ones in existence, with the exception of a very imperfect one in the possession of Mr. Ralph Munroe, commodore of the Biscayne Bay Yacht Club, at Cocoanut Grove. The present local habitat of the *Crocodilus Americanus* extends from the north end of Biscayne Bay to Cape Sable. The group Crocodilus is divided into (1) Crocodiles ; (2) Alligators. Of the crocodiles there are many varieties, some of which are most interesting. I will give the general characteristics and habitat of those that are known.

Gavialis Gangeticus.

It is remarkable for its long narrow snout. The two lower front teeth, and, skipping two teeth, the next ones back, run into orifices in the upper jaw. They attain a length of from twenty-five to thirty feet.

Habitat.—Hindostan, Malabar, Ganges River.

Crocodilus Acutus.

This reptile was first described by Alexander von Humboldt. It lies in wait along the trails that lead through the jungle and attacks many small quadrupeds, even the jaguar. They attain the length of eighteen feet.

Habitat.—South America, West Indies, Ecuador, New Granada, Venezuela, Yucatan, Guatemala, Cuba, San Domingo, Jamaica, Martinique, Margarita.

Crocodilus Bipocratus.

Very wide, smooth saddle across the shoulders. Color, yellowish green, with dark blotches. A long, pointed snout, with two high parallel ridges running from the eye formed of bones. Back of the head is a group of six heavy plates. Length, thirty feet.

Habitat.—South Asia, Sunda River, from Ceylon to New Ireland.

Crocodilus Vulgaris
(the Crocodile of the Nile).

Four plates in pairs behind the head; six plates in pairs on the neck. The plates on the back vary in number in individuals, but are usually from fifteen to sixteen. On the tail, eighteen pairs and twenty single plates. The color is a bronze-green, with small black blotches on the back. The sides and belly are of a dirty yellow, with dark blotches, but on the back these blotches vary with the individual. Length, twenty to thirty feet.

Habitat.—All the big rivers in Africa, especially the Nile and the rivers near Madagascar.

Crocodilus Frontatus
(or Short-Bodied Crocodile).

It is distinguished by its high head, short forehead, and broad snout, which is very blunt. The nose is slightly turned up. High bone ridges extend over the eyes. The swimming ligaments between the toes are very short. The head is dark in color, and light-brown ridges extend over the back. Length, fifteen to twenty feet. Paul du Chaillu (the discoverer of the gorilla and the pigmies) brought the first specimens of this crocodile to the United States.

Habitat.—Africa, from seven degrees north to fourteen degrees south latitude.

CROCODILUS POROSUS.

This crocodile resembles very much the *Crocodilus Bipocratus*, having the two ridges running from the eye to the end of the snout, but is slightly different in color, being of an even gray tint.

Habitat.—India.

CROCODILUS PALUSTRIS.

The jaw is of moderate width and well arched. Color, gray with black blotches. Probably attains a larger size than any of the Crocodilia, one now in the possession of the British Museum being thirty-three feet in length.

Habitat.—India, Australia (where it is called the marsh crocodile).

Across the Everglades

CROCODILUS MARGINATUS
(or Marginal Crocodile).

This species differs from the North African crocodile by a curious concavity of the forehead and its stronger dorsal plate.

CROCODILUS AMERICANUS.

This crocodile is akin to *Crocodilus Acutus*, which it most closely resembles. The head is low, snout long and narrow, with two well-defined arches on the upper jaw. The teeth are long and narrow, the ivory being very white. The two front lower ones protrude through holes in the upper jaw. In some specimens but a single one of these come through, though I think these cases are rare and probably occurred from the malformation of one of the teeth.

On the back of the neck is a group of high ridges, back of which is a wide, smooth saddle. Four rows of ridges extend half-way down the tail, the two outer ones extending to the end. The hind legs are very powerful, but the body is usually slimmer than that of the alligator. The color is of a greenish gray, lighter on the belly, with black blotches all over the body.

It is much more active and savage than the alligator. I have known one to attack a boat and, closing its powerful jaws, take a piece of wood out of her bow ; with great difficulty it was despatched with a rifle.

Habitat.—The Southeast Atlantic coast of Florida.

CROCODILUS CALAPHACTUS
(called the False Crocodile).

CROCODILUS INTERMEDIUS.

Habitat.—Orinoco.

This crocodile differs from the *Crocodilus Americanus* by having a more slender snout and the plates on the back more nearly uniform.

CROCODILUS ROBUSTUS.

Habitat.—Madagascar.

CROCODILUS RHOMBIFER.

Habitat.—Central America.

CROCODILUS MORELETI.

Habitat.—Guatemala.

CROCODILUS JOHNSTONI.

Habitat.—Australia.

CROCODILUS CATAPHRACTUS.

Habitat.—West Africa.

Following are the characteristics and habitat of several varieties of alligator:

ALLIGATOR SCELEROPS.

Snout broad, articulations running in rows from the head to the tail. High ridges over the eyes. Color black, light yellow on the belly.

Habitat.—East Brazil, Buenos Ayres, Peru.

ALLIGATOR NIGER
(called the Moorish Cayman).

The characteristic is five rows of plates around the neck. Color, black. Belly, yellowish white.

Habitat.—North Brazil, Bolivia, Peru, Ecuador, North Peru, the Amazon River.

Across the Everglades

CAMPSA LUCIUS
(the North American Alligator).

This alligator is akin to the South American varieties. The snout is broad, body heavy, eyes prominent, and protected by ridges. Articulations running in rows down the back. Color black, yellowish white on the belly. Teeth, yellow ivory, thick and strong.

Habitat.—South Carolina, Georgia, Mississippi, Louisiana, Florida.

CHAPTER IV

Land of the Big Snake—Florida Sponges—Crawfish—An
Unlucky Dive—Amateur Surgery—Cape Sable—The
Edge of the Everglades.

WITH an apology for my slight digression, we will return to our coasting trip and our unsuccessful crocodile hunt on Card Sound. I had originally intended to hunt crocodile for a few days more, but, knowing the water in the Everglades would be getting lower as the month advanced, I considered it prudent to push south, locating well where the largest crocodile lived, intending to return in March for a systematic hunt after my winter's work in the Everglades had been accomplished.

On the 31st of December we got the "Cupid" under way and ran as far as the mouth of Jew-Fish Creek. This creek is nothing but a very narrow passage, which connects Barnes Sound with Black Water Sound. I am using here the names as given by the Geodetic Coast Survey Chart. Barnes Sound is known to the natives as Little Card Sound, and the northeast end of Florida Bay is called by them Barnes Sound. Comparatively little is known of these sounds, especially the northwest shores, as the few people who live on Key Largo and the smaller keys use the better water communication of the Hawk Channel for the transportation of their produce. Jew-Fish Creek has rather a blind entrance, which passes through a heavy growth of mangroves.

The water is quite deep and the current runs through with great swiftness, and is a fine place for all kinds of fish. The channel divides into two or three branches, the one running nearest Key Largo being the best. With a light wind we sailed across Blackwater Sound, which is a pretty sheet of water nearly circular, and about four miles in diameter, taking a course nearly west, in order to find the opening which leads into the Bay of Florida, called Boggy Creek, a rather difficult place to get a sail-boat through, as the bottom is so soft that a pole pushes in to its full length.

There is a second opening to this bay, more to the northwest, which runs into several small land-locked bays. After much difficulty we succeeded in getting through " Boggy," and anchored for the night near its opening into the Bay of Florida. From here I took a westerly course, which was somewhat out of my way, in order to reconnoitre the uninhabited northwest shore of this large bay, and also to prove the accuracy of a statement made by Ed. Brewer, that a year and a half ago, while hunting on a certain creek, he had killed a great snake of a kind that he had never seen before. This creek leads nearly to the Everglades. Brewer believed that he could take me to the very spot, and thought that perhaps I might find others of the same variety. I have for a long time believed that in the southern part of Florida there exists a snake of immense size. What this snake is has been my longing desire to discover.

Many absurd and sensational stories have been circulated this winter, without any truth in them whatever, concerning the capture of this huge reptile. A circus charlatan brought a python down from the North in a box. He disappeared for a few days, and returned to the settlement with a twelve-pound snake in a bag, that he claimed to have captured on Long Key, which is in the Everglades. I am quite sure that without an Indian guide this man never reached that spot alone. But the fraud was quite successful, and the newspapers were completely taken in. Taking the sloop along the northwest shore as far as the water would permit, Brewer and I left the " Cupid" in charge of Sam, and with the " Coacochee" started for the " Land of the Big Snake."

Leaving the main part of the bay, we entered a smaller one, which we crossed, and with unerring accuracy Brewer steered for what appeared to be a solid wall of trees; but on reaching it a hole in the foliage was seen, from which a fresh-water stream was issuing. The water was perfectly clear, and just after entering I could see many fish. Reaching for my light spear, I soon landed three fresh-water garfish. Continuing farther up the stream, the foliage became more tangled and made our progress very slow, until we reached what seemed to be the head of canoe navigation. The scene would rival some of those depicted on the Amazon River. The hanging vines, the tropical foliage, obscured nearly all light, and the air had an earthy, snaily smell.

Brewer, who had been pulling the canoe along by the overhanging branches, stopped and said, " We are near the place where I killed the snake." I immediately felt for my revolver, thinking there might be a whole den of pythons somewhere in the vicinity, that had come to the funeral of their progenitor. The place itself was certainly the snakiest one I have ever been in. Brewer crawled on shore, with his head to the ground, and began lifting up the rotten leaves, examining everything very carefully. This search continued for nearly half an hour, when he said, " I have got it, but the buzzards have scattered the bones pretty bad." I jumped out of the canoe at once and joined him, all eagerness, to find a skeleton that might have belonged to the strange variety I have been in search of. Under the first layer of leaves was a section of vertebra, evidently that of a snake ; its diameter, as compared with snakes I had usually seen, seemed very large. By clearing a space of ten feet around, we uncovered more pieces of the backbone and a great number of ribs. I returned to the canoe for a pail, and after a long period of careful work we recovered more than two-thirds of the entire body, but nothing as yet of the head, that I was so anxious to find ; among the last two pieces, however, I discovered a bit of the jaw, with a large fang sticking in it.

That fang told me much, as I could plainly

see the capillary tube running through it, which indicated to me rattlesnake. I did not, however, wish to decide hurriedly as to this fact, and preferred to wait until I had assembled the bones into the full structure, at the University of Pennsylvania, in consultation with the professors skilled in osteology. I got Brewer to tell me again of the killing of this reptile, a year and a half ago. It seems he had been hunting and exploring up this creek, in order to find a canoe passage that would lead to the Everglades. Pushing his way through the thick foliage, as we had done, he saw a little way ahead of him, on the low limb of a tree, what seemed to be the largest snake he had ever seen in his life. The snake he describes as having longitudinal stripes, and not looking like a rattler. To pick up his shot-gun and fire was the work of a second. The snake was badly riddled. He approached with the idea of despatching him and taking his skin, when he was overpowered by a strong, sickening smell, which caused him great sickness of the stomach and faintness. He lay in a partly unconscious condition for some time, and when he recovered sufficiently, he reached his canoe and made his way to the coast without paying any more attention to the snake. On my return to the North, this skeleton was carefully put together, and it was decided that it had belonged to a rattlesnake, but the formation of the vertebræ seemed to be different from those of the usual variety of the Florida rattler, which may account for the observation Brewer had made of the longitudinal stripes. In life it would have been about eight feet in length.

That great snakes of some species do exist in Florida, yet to be discovered, I have not the slightest doubt. I pin my faith to the account that two different Indians have given me of snakes that were at least eighteen feet in length, and evidently belonged to the constrictor family. As I have remarked before, I have never found a Seminole to lie. I did not explore the head of this creek, but I am under the impression that it reaches to within two miles of the Everglades.

With our successful find we paddled back to the " Cupid," and on reaching open water found that it was blowing very fresh, and a tough splashing paddle we had of it. I immediately took two reefs in the mainsail, and squared away for Whaleback Key, to the leeward of which we anchored for the night. On the coast chart the Bay of Florida is quite accurately put down, but there are a countless number of shallow bays to the northwest, some of them quite large, the outlines of which have not been attempted, and as the water is so shoal that nothing but the lightest-draught canoe can float, the probabilities are that they have never all been explored.

On the 2d of January we got under way with a stiff southeaster, and beat up to the Key Largo shore, finding a snug little harbor back of Hammer Point, where we went ashore to do a little reconnoitring. Key Largo is one of the most fertile of the Florida Keys. It has not very much soil to boast of, but what there is is exceedingly rich and lies in pockets in the coralline rock. At one time there was quite a lot of valuable wood growing, but the settlers have made sad inroads upon it. Small trees of mahogany, crab-wood, lignum-vitæ, and satinwood are still to be seen. This island, considering the comparatively few people that are on it, ships during the year a great many tropical fruits and vegetables to the Northern market, the pineapple doing very well. The houses are all on the southeast side of the island, and have their little docks on the Hawk Channel, where small steamers and sail-boats can stop for freight. The people are industrious, intelligent, and very hospitable to strangers.

Crossing the island from the Bay of Florida is rather difficult, as there are no roads, and the very blind trails, which seem to be little used, have to cross several swampy places. A short time after our return to the yacht, a skiff containing two young men came alongside; they had been fishing for crawfish, and had quite a boat-load; they threw a quantity on deck, and seemed offended when pay was offered them. They gave me information as to where the best fishing-grounds could be found. The crawfish is much like our Northern lobster, but has a more delicate flavor and the shell is thinner. Instead of the large claws, it has feelers that are quite thick at the base, and more like the shrimp. The shell is rougher than that of the lobster, and there is more red in the variegated color. They average in weight about a pound and a half, though one we caught weighed four.

I found these men had been using fish-spears. After they had left us, with various information about Key Largo, Sam and I started off for a good supply of fresh provisions. We hunted in vain for the home of the crawfish, but at last, after rounding a point in about two feet of water, the bottom seemed to be alive with them, and in less than one hour, with a spear, I landed in my canoe two hundred pounds of these delicious shell-fish. On returning to the "Cupid" we had a splendid dinner, after which we salted down the remaining fish, which the following day we sun-dried. A good-sized bundle of these I carried into the Everglades, and, by soaking a couple overnight, had many a palatable breakfast.

Nearly all these bays and sounds abound in sponges, the gathering of which is a great industry of the people of the Bahama Islands and the Florida Keys, Key West being the great market for their sale, entirely by the method of auction. Sponges are taken on the coral banks, in various depths of water, by diving or by means of the sponge-hook. A sponge-hook is a curved iron with three prongs, into the socket of which is fitted a very long pole. The hook is thrown over the sponge (located with the water-glass), which by a quick jerk is loosened from its root and brought to the surface.

The water-glass is the constant companion of the fishermen here, and usually consists of a bucket whose bottom has been replaced by a sheet of glass. It is curious to how many different purposes they put this glass. I have watched with great amusement two darkies fishing for large fish, one looking down into the water, the other with the line in his hand. The darky with the water-glass would sing out, "Pull," as soon as he would see the hook disappear in a fish's mouth; his companion would haul in, perhaps, a thirty-pound mutton-fish. The appearance of a sponge when taken from the bottom is not the light, springy, soft, yellow-colored affair that we are accustomed to. The general shape is similar, but the surface is smooth, with the exception of a few sharp volcano-like craters on the top; in color as black as your hat, and to the touch like soft india-rubber.

Like the anemone, it has life like a fish, but grows to the bottom like a plant. What annoys the sponge-fisherman is, that he sees so many sponges of different kinds before he meets one that is marketable. The largest of the worthless kind is the "Loggerhead." This sponge is on the bottom in enormous quantities. It is the shape of a round life-preserver, and sometimes attains the diameter of five feet.

Then there is the potato-sponge, and several curious varieties which have sharp spines through them, that hurt the hands very badly when pressed. Neptune's cup is also another variety. These sponges are known at a long distance by the expert, and are passed by, but the beginner is apt to bring many to the surface before he recognizes them. The sponges that are marketable are the glove, sheep's-wool, grass, and yellow. These vary somewhat among themselves in quality.

I have a sheep's-wool in my possession that is larger than my head, but so soft that I can put it in my closed hand and it cannot be seen.

Sponge-fishing and the examination of the wonderful marine life on the coral bottom through the glass has always had a great fascination for me, and my fondness for sponge-diving caused the only accident that occurred to me during the winter. While at our anchorage, near Hammer Point, Sam expressed his desire to take a paddle in one of the canoes, so I pushed off with him in the " Hissee." Sam is a good sailor and oarsman, but the quick motion of the narrower boat was too much for his accuracy of balance and we had not proceeded far before he made a quick side movement that capsized the canoe, throwing us both into the water. I righted the canoe, and after baling her out we returned to the " Cupid," which was not far away. Regaining the deck, I took off my wet clothes, and while undressing I saw on the bottom a sponge that seemed a good one, and, wishing to prolong my bath, prepared to make a dive. I was perfectly well aware that we were anchored in about five feet of water, and that a flat dive was necessary, but I had not noticed that in taking off my clothes I had made the deck very wet and slippery, and just before jumping my feet went from under me backward. I entered the water in nearly a vertical position, and struck the bottom just at a place where there was a sharp piece of coral sticking up. This made a gash in my forehead and cut half-way through the bone of my nose like a knife, with a smaller slit running nearly to the end. With great difficulty I regained the deck, with the help of the two men, for I was greatly stunned by the blow and had swallowed a great deal of salt-water. A quantity of blood was running down my chest, and a terrible spectacle I must have presented, as I could see by the expression on the faces of my two companions.

Across the Everglades

I said to Sam, "If I am going to have any nose the rest of my life, you and Brewer must assist me in a little surgery. Hand me the bag that contains my surgical case."

He did this as quickly as possible. I selected a flesh needle of the proper size, then drew from the bottle the medium carbolized sinew, with which I threaded the needle. Washing the wound with fresh water, I felt the parts carefully to see where the stitches were to go. I told Sam that I depended on him to make a good flat knot and drive the needle through where I directed him, as light stitches might pull out and would be of no use. I told him that I was suffering very little, that the pain would come to-morrow, that he must not be unnerved by the amount of blood, and that I could lose much more, and that without fainting. So we set to work, and in a short time completed a good bit of amateur surgery, which has been pronounced by a skilful surgeon as good a piece of work as could have been done under the most favorable circumstances at home.

I have always been very grateful to Sam for his efficient aid, for, blinded with blood, without his eyes and hands I could have done but little, and we were a hundred miles away from a doctor. Brewer helped also as much as he could, and did quick work in getting me out of the water. It seems strange how one accident is so often followed by another. First the upsetting of the canoe, then my unfortunate dive. Some of the people in Miami had insisted that the Everglade business was merely a blind; that our real destination was Cuba. If they could have seen me at this time, they would have been certain that I had been fighting for Cuba's freedom.

We got under way the next morning and ran through a very narrow channel between two banks, but the sun, being in the right direction, helped us very much. By running by the color of the water, one becomes quite expert after a while in judging the depth. Leaving Cotton Key and Bird Bush on our left, we took a course which led us between Upper and Lower Matecumbe Islands, into the Hawk Channel, in order to avoid some very shoal water, that stretches across the Bay of Florida almost to the main land.

In the opening between the two islands we very soon sighted Indian Key. It was on this Key that Dr. Perrine was killed by the Indians during the Seminole War, and his children so miraculously escaped by hiding in a turtle-pen. The island is high, with deep water around it, and has about ten acres of good land. We landed on the northeast end of Lower Matecumbe to take a stroll among the cocoanut-trees and allay our thirst with the cool milk, which was a great relief from our barrelled water.

After dinner we skirted the shore of Lower Matecumbe and swung sharply round the point, dodging the banks, to a snug little anchorage for the night. The wound in my face was doing well; my nose felt about two inches wide. As it was originally of generous proportions, I was a little curious as to the ultimate result.

On the 4th of January, after a comfortable breakfast of crawfish and green turtle, we shaped our course for Cape Sable. The detour to Lower Matecumbe Island was necessary in order to avoid the very shoal water that extends over the east end of the Bay of Florida. Carefully feeling our way through the gaps between the banks, with a light wind, we made very good headway. At noon, having a good natural horizon, I took a meridian altitude for practice, to see how my instruments were working, and

Across the Everglades

made out my latitude and longitude within a mile and a half of what the chart gave, determined by cross bearings on known islands.

We reached Cape Sable (Southeast Cape) early in the afternoon, and came to anchor near a small schooner loaded with wood. Brewer and I took a canoe and landed on the extreme point. The first thing I saw was the skull of what must have been a turtle of enormous size; it was white and water-worn, eleven inches wide and a foot long. I threw it at once into the canoe, that we had hauled upon the beach, thinking it would make a pleasant souvenir of the most southerly point of the United States, to put in my den. We walked around the point along a very pretty sand beach, and watched the shark and tarpon that were occasionally rising to the surface. About a mile from where we were a large bunch of cocoanut-trees reached to the water's edge. This is a part of a plantation that was started many years ago, but the people who lived there had deserted it. We examined an old house which had signs of being occupied by a darky, but no one was in sight. There was an air of desolation about the place, and, looking out upon the Gulf, not a sail could be seen.

Across the Everglades

On returning to the " Cupid" I received a hail from an old man on the wood schooner (that we had supposed was without a crew), asking me if I could send a boat ashore to get two of his men, who had been cutting wood, as they had no small boat, and otherwise would have to swim. I immediately despatched Brewer in the " Coacochee." When he returned from his errand I took the canoe to make a visit. I found a very dilapidated old craft about fifty feet long that was leaking badly. The captain had evidently looked upon us with a great deal of suspicion, having mistaken us for Cuban filibusters. Can it be wondered at? My own appearance at this time must have intensified this idea. I was sunburned to the color of old mahogany, and had a cross bandage over my forehead and nose. He implored me to let him have a little sugar and coffee, as they were in an almost starving condition, the food having given out two weeks before; his men had been delayed in getting the lumber out, also by the mosquitoes that had infested the place where they were chopping to such an extent that one man nearly lost his life. Their faces and hands certainly bore evidence to the truth of this statement. I gladdened the old man's heart by sending him a good supply of coffee, sugar, tobacco, and some of our salted crawfish.

It was not long before I saw the smoke of a pine-knot fire started in his sand-box on deck. We got under way the next morning and surveyed a channel along shore some fifteen miles to the eastward, finding six feet of water, where the Coast Survey Chart marks one. I carefully made up my corrections for future use, as I found some splendid tarpon ground. On Wednesday, January 6, we started with a heavy northeaster and ran for Cape Sable; on rounding it the wind veered to the northwest, and three reefs and bobbed jib were in order. All day we thrashed to windward against a heavy sea, which kept us working at the pump constantly. After getting by the Northwest Cape the wind stopped a little and we were enabled to gain ground. The heavy squalls would strike so hard and so quickly that I became very much exhausted with the steering, but did not like to turn back, as I believed that towards afternoon the heaviest wind would be over, which proved to be the case, and I knew that as soon as we could get a little farther up the coast we would have good harbors to depend on. Early in the afternoon we were abreast of what is known as Shark River. Why Shark River is not easy to decide, for it is merely an opening among the many that lead through the Ten Thousand Islands Archipelago. The real mouths of the Shark and Harney Rivers are about fifteen miles back of the islands. Taking this opening, we ran into perfectly smooth water, letting go our anchor to cook and have a rest. Very few people ever travel among these islands, and many have lost their way and almost starved to death. The shore appearance is very deceptive. It would be supposed such very large trees could only be supported by hard deep soil, but such is not the case. On landing on some of the islands, we found them to be low and covered with two varieties of mangrove, the trees having large trunks and growing to the height of from fifty to sixty feet. By jumping on the ground you can shake it for many yards. It seems to consist of nothing but a mass of floating roots. These islands cover an area of about seventy-five miles by fifty.

The Geodetic Chart merely indicates the edges lying on the Gulf of Mexico, and has attempted nothing of the inside work ; no surveys of any kind have been made. I soon discovered that all the data given in the land-maps were entirely erroneous. The lack of knowledge of the depth of water existing here had been of great disadvantage in working out certain problems at the Naval War College. I had decided before leaving home that, could I spare the time from the main object of my trip, I would carefully sound out and familiarize myself with some of the channels through this labyrinth, which would permit me to pilot a torpedo-boat or fleet of boats operating on the coast. As this matter is somewhat confidential in its nature, I will omit mention of the time occupied by my hydrographic work and take up my narrative at the mouth of the Harney River, which as the crow flies is nine miles from the Gulf.

The water here became perfectly fresh, and as we ascended the current got stronger. The bottom is formed of coralline limestone and is smooth, but higher up the character of the rock is jagged, so much so that a mile before reaching the source in the Everglades we were brought to a stand-still and cast anchor. Here I decided on making my first Everglade station, and the next day, taking my instruments and an axe ashore,

Across the Everglades

I made a clearing, and with my sextant and artificial horizon took a meridian altitude. In the afternoon I decided to make a preliminary reconnoissance of the rest of the river and cut out timber in order to let our loaded canoes pass. Sam had never seen the Everglades, and begged to be taken along, that he might judge of our wisdom in trying to cross to the Atlantic. After a good dinner, Brewer, Sam, and I started up the stream, which at this point was not more than fifty feet wide. The rough, rock formation of the bottom still continued, the banks approaching each other gradually until, after paddling three-quarters of a mile, the foliage met overhead and we were obliged to lie in the bottom of the canoe, dragging her along the narrow water-way, that was hardly wider than our beam.

Here we found for the first time that we were on a travelled Indian route. The fallen trees and branches had been cut out just the right width to admit of the passing of a canoe; some cuts must have been made many years ago, while others were evidently made within the year. The water still ran swiftly. Just before entering the tangle of vines we surprised two wood-ibis, that I thought might prove edible. The range was not more than thirty yards, and I killed them both with a well-directed right and left from the shot-gun. But a little way farther and an opening appeared, letting in a flood of daylight, and we suddenly burst into the pathless Everglades. Here was the source of the Harney River very closely defined. We were standing on the rim that dams up that great basin of shoal water, with so few outlets that except in very dry seasons it cannot drain itself. What a sea of grass! What was there beyond that horizon before reaching the shore of the Atlantic? Did those wonderfully fertile islands exist, the secret of which is so strictly guarded by the Seminole from the white man? Were great springs and lakes to be found as the main supply of all this water, which cannot alone be accounted for by the rainfall? Does yonder horizon cover the land of the Big Snake? These and many other questions presented themselves as I gazed upon that apparently limitless grassy sea.

The silence was broken by Sam, who said, " I am glad I have seen this; it looks like a mighty hard place to travel in, and I can easily see how people have lost their way in going a mile. I think *I* can get back to Miami by the

coast a month or so before *you* are heard of."
A few small scattered islands can be seen to the
east close by; to the southeast a line of trees
which define the edge of the Glades. About a
mile from us is the source of the Shark River,
in which the water is not so deep as the Harney. The Indians seldom use it for canoe-
travel. The Harney River also strikes a better
point, from which the Big Cypress can be
reached to the north. Along the edge of the
Big Cypress Swamp is a favorite place for the
Indians to hunt the otter.

Before leaving Miami I had seen Robert
Osceola in his canoe, who had just come across
the Everglades with nineteen otter-hides, to sell
at the trading-post. He said, "All Indians
over Big Cypress; big otter-hunt; stay good
while." I was glad to hear this, for it was just
as well that they should not know that I was
penetrating into what they consider is their
country, and if they should see any of my
scientific instruments they would jump at the
conclusion that I was employed by the government, and (though they will probably never
raise their hand against the white man again)
might make things unpleasant.

With the northeasterly route intended, it was

not probable that we should meet any Indians,
even if we should pass their camps; and upon
these great winter hunts they are always accompanied by their squaws and children. As I
knew, from the experience of others, how useless it was to obtain any travelling information
from them, my wish was, if possible, that they
should not even know that I was in the Everglades. If I had started from Miami, this
would have been impossible, as some of their
runners would have been encountered, and in a
week all the Indians in South Florida would
have known that "Willie Bee," as they had
named me, who usually travelled in one of their
canoes, was going to try and cross the Everglades. Not meeting any Indians on the coast,
my start and my entrance into the Glades by
the Harney River was unknown to them.

After taking a short rest we retraced our
steps through the hole in the wall of tropical
foliage, where the river starts, and, the current
aiding us greatly, we soon reached the sloop.
It was getting so late in the afternoon that
taking photographs seemed rather uncertain, but
as we were to make our start the next day in
the canoes, it would be my last chance to get
a picture of the "Cupid." This negative, as I

feared, turned out under-exposed. The photographs taken with my three-and-a-half-square film camera, to illustrate this book, have proved fairly good, considering that some of the choicest bits I had wished to reproduce were usually caught late in the afternoon, and our starts were made before the sun rose in the morning. Films are never as satisfactory as dry plates. I regretted very much that economy in weight and the liability to breakage forbade my using them.

The night proved very cool, the minimum registering thermometer showing 42.5°, a stiff norther having blown during the night. This meant a killing frost for North Florida. Early on the morning of the 9th we began sorting the outfit to go in the canoes, leaving on board the " Cupid" a good supply of groceries for her return trip, taking a good bundle of salted crawfish, a gallon can of kerosene for each canoe, a brush-hook, two Newhouse traps, two cheese-cloth mosquito-bars, and my Maine woods axe, the only things added to the outfit already described. We divided the load between the two canoes, the grocery-chest going in my boat and the cooking-chest in Brewer's. When completely loaded up I found that the canoes were

not in the least overweighted, and would naturally get lighter as we progressed. After bidding
Sam adieu and giving him a letter to mail at
Miami (written on a piece of wrapping-paper),
at half-past nine I gave the order to shove off.

CHAPTER V

Fighting Saw-Grass—The Limpkin—Making Camps—
Sweet Water—Long Key—A Meridian Altitude—
Willoughby Key—The Cabbage-Palm.

OUR reconnoissance of the previous day helped us very much in the ascent of the river. It was not very long before we emerged from the woods, on the edge of the Everglades, where we made a halt to give me time to adjust the bicycle wheel to my canoe and get my field-book, pencil, and compass ready to take my courses and lay down my distance. Brewer has a way of his own in figuring miles by the number of poles required. I told him to make an independent calculation on each distance run, which would give me a third check on my own work ; it was always a surprise to me how his crude reckoning tallied with my cyclometer. My general plan was to take a distant object as a sub-station, and when it was reached to work up my dead reckoning to it, then at noon, whenever an opportunity offered, to take a meridian altitude with my sextant to more accurately establish my latitude and longitude. There seems to be plenty of water, and most of the leads have been good, enabling me to go in a northeasterly direction, but much dodging around is necessary, to avoid heavy bunches of grass, of which about three varieties are encountered. First, the matted, half-floating grass, which where the water is low gives some trouble and hard pushing, but ordinarily is not noticed. Secondly, the round grass, which is more abundant on the eastern edge. Thirdly, the saw-grass, which is the worst of all.

When the rock is near the surface, with little soil, this saw-grass grows to a height of about four feet, but where the soil is deeper it has very little water around its roots and reaches a height of ten feet. This is the great barrier to Everglade travel; it pays better to go twenty-five miles around than half a mile through. What makes this grass so formidable and so much to be dreaded is the saw-like edge with which it is armed on three sides. If you get a blade between your hand and the pole, it will cut you to the bone, with a jagged gash that takes long to heal. The nose and face suffer much. When very thick, pushing through it becomes almost impossible. To cut it down ahead leaves a short stubble that spikes the canoe. The best method is to push from the stern, your feet and legs protected by rubber hip-boots, the canoe dividing the grass on either side ahead. If, however, you should have very much of this to do, the upper parts of the boots will be cut through. This happened to me once, but I had repair cloth and cement, with which I mended them. Game was very plentiful on the edge of the Glades, but as we advanced to the interior it became less abundant. But having found deer a long way from solid land, we hoped to come across them again. We saw the white egret (plume birds) in every direction. On a little island that we passed, about twenty feet long, was the nest of a blue heron, with young ones about a week old. Two large ducks flew up ahead of us, which were about the size of brant, and are of a variety peculiar to the Everglades; they are very good eating. A bird which we became intimately acquainted with later on, and which we then saw for the first time, was the limpkin (suborder, Ralli; family Aramidæ; genus, Aramus; species, Aramus Giganteus).

If an English snipe were three feet high he

would look very much like this bird. In fact, the resemblance was so great that I had no hesitation in cooking and eating the first that I shot, and found them really very good, especially some of the younger birds. The limpkin is a native of Florida, where it breeds freely. It is also found in Central America and the West India Islands. Authorities state that it was once a very abundant species, but is now seldom seen, except in the less inhabited districts. Brewer drew my attention to two birds soaring quite a distance off; he said they were the Everglade kite, and are found nowhere else; he had a standing order to kill some, and was anxious to get a shot, but they are difficult to approach. They look like a small hen-hawk, with rather darker plumage. To collectors a single egg of this bird is worth ten dollars. The same price is also paid for a good skin.

There must be thousands of otter in this vicinity, for their trails crossed each other in all directions, and wherever there was a little dry ground their fresh slides of the night before could be observed. We had no serious setbacks to our travel, but the water was not as high in the Glades as I should have liked to have seen it. A good rain might have given us an extra inch or two, but we did not get it. Being obliged to stop every little while to get compass-bearings and calculate distances retarded us very much, but I was determined to spend all the time on this work that was necessary, as any grave error at the start would have thrown things badly out at the other end. The same care was given throughout the trip to the very last mile ; at no time did I allow myself to become hurried. A little before noon we crossed a fresh Indian canoe trail, less than a week old. It led to the north, and we supposed that the owner was on his way to join the hunt on the Big Cypress.

I preferred not to sleep in the canoes unless absolutely forced to do so, and made it a practice after three o'clock not to pass any little island without examination for dry ground, which was evidently getting rarer as we journeyed on. At four in the afternoon we passed a little bunch of bushes, which I sent Brewer in to investigate ; he reported that we might clear a piece seven or eight feet long that would be dry enough, and, there being nothing in sight that looked more promising, we proceeded to make camp with brush-hook and axe.

Places were cleared for the two canoes, and after unloading them they were placed bottom up.

The little spot of ground was not large enough to spread the tent, so the fly alone was used ; sticks were cut for the cheese-cloths and the blankets unrolled. No fire could be made here, so we started the kettle boiling on the kerosene-stove, and in a very short time had cocoa, cumpti, and crackers ready. Supper over, we enjoyed a good smoke, and I began by the light of the lantern to plot my course on my chart and work up my reckoning, calling this camp Station No. 2. I found that in a straight line we had covered eight miles and a quarter, but the path of the canoe was nineteen miles long. This was quite as good as I expected to make, in fact, better, as I surely thought that the daily rate would be reduced to five miles when we got into heavier work. Several very good leads were met, in which the boats made good progress, and the water was in all places clear, even where the grass was thick, with a mile and a half current setting to the southwest ; rocky bottom was found frequently near the surface, with no mud on it ; then again the mud was from two inches to a foot thick.

Across the Everglades

The popular impression has always been that the Everglades is a huge swamp, full of malaria and disease germs. There was certainly nothing in our surroundings that would remind one of a swamp. Around the shores of the little islands the mud may be a trifle soft, but pure water is running over it, and no stagnant pools can be found. In the daytime the cool breeze has an undisturbed sweep, and the water is protected from overheating by the shade the grass affords. Water-plants of various kinds and several varieties of fish and reptiles keep the balance of life, as in a self-sustaining aquarium. As will be seen by the analysis, this water is quite wholesome to drink. As would naturally be supposed, it is rather hard, as much of it comes out of and flows over the coralline limestone.

I had no hesitation in drinking it whenever the canoe stopped, taking two or three glasses at a time, when thirsty from the exertion of poling. It agreed with Brewer and myself perfectly; we did not know a sick hour from this or any other cause. After working for about an hour and a half, I undressed and crawled into my sleeping-bag, not forgetting the very important task of winding my watch

and the two chronometers. I expected of
course to drop off quickly to sleep, as I was
just comfortably tired by the day's work. But
I had reckoned without my host. Everything
had been so desolate and quiet during the day
that one would naturally think that the still-
ness of the night would be quite appalling.
But as the hours advanced new combinations
of sounds broke on the ear, until it seemed
that a menagerie had arrived and all the ani-
mals were exercising their lungs. From whence
could all these noises come, a few only of which
I could recognize? The first to tune up were
the frogs. These frogs do not have the respect-
able croak of their Northern brothers, which is
rather soothing to the nerves than otherwise ;
they make a noise like a creeky sheave in an
old block, the pitch of which is in direct ratio
to the size of the frog. But the worst sound
to sleep through is the cry of the limpkin.
When do these birds sleep? or do they ever
sleep? We have seen them about all day, and
they seemed like a quiet, well-behaved bird, but
their conduct at night is something most dis-
reputable. I would drop off into a doze, con-
quering the other sounds, but as soon as a
limpkin would screech I would be wide awake

at once. The mosquitoes at Station No. 2 had been rather bad, possibly because we were not yet far enough from the coast, as I expected immunity from these pests when we were well in the interior. There is no harbor for them from the wind but the tall grass, and the water is not stagnant for their larvæ.

We turned out early and cooked a simple breakfast of coffee, oatmeal, and crawfish. Thinking it better to do the cooking for the day as much as possible in the morning, I boiled a pot of potatoes, of which we had a good supply. The oatmeal, with condensed milk poured out of the can, was especially good, and we felt in fighting trim for the day. Loading the canoes with exactly the same articles they contained yesterday, I took a last look around the little patch of ground which we called camp, lest anything should be forgotten. After deciding on my course and spending a short time on my field-book, we struck a good water-lead and made very good headway at first, but the difficulties of Everglade travel soon made themselves apparent. The good water-leads came to an end, many of them heading up in big saw-grass, beyond which we could see nothing that could float a canoe. Sometimes reaching within a quarter of a mile of the little object that my sights were taken to, I would be compelled to return to my starting-point and make a departure, with perhaps little better success than the first time. Game was very plentiful; deer were started frequently, but the swinging of the pole from a standing position would take them out of range, and there would be no chance of shooting one. To hunt successfully would have required a whole day, and I could not make use of an entire deer; that, indeed, would have been the kind of waste that I have so much condemned in other hunters. Both canoes were loaded as much as I wished them to be, and even if the game became very scarce I had no fear of starving, having portable food with me enough to last two months.

At the end of a long stretch of low grass a beautiful sight presented itself: seven deer were feeding in about four inches of water. We had the wind of them, and got rather closer than usual. The sight of a white man was strange to them, and if we had been seated in our canoes could no doubt have gone very close to them. A little way ahead from here we saw some cormorants and blue heron. On ap-

proaching we found quite a large " rookery ;"
most of the birds were laying, so we took
quite a supply of cormorant and blue heron
eggs, with which I intended to make omelets.
A few Everglade terrapins and a fresh-water
turtle, about a foot long, were seen to-day ;
also some of the flat, soft-shell turtle. Both
these varieties the Seminoles eat ; they usually
broil them in their shells before the fire. The
water seemed all to be moving in a southwesterly direction, over a more broken rocky formation. Sometimes pools would be crossed
eight or ten feet wide and five feet deep. These
would look like a pretty aquarium, with its
growth of water-plants and its picturesque rock
bottom, through which big-mouthed bass eight
or ten inches long could be seen swimming.
Occasionally, in the centre of these pools, a
dark hole a few inches in diameter could be
seen ; down one of these I could push my pole
to a long distance, and the water was coming
out from it with quite a little head. They
are to be found all over the Everglades, and
are, I believe, one of its greatest water-sup-
plies.

All this moving water cannot be accounted
for by the rain alone, and the water is too hard

for rain-water, so that in all probability more comes from below than above. Serpent life seems to abound; many moccasins were passed, but we comforted ourselves that we would meet few rattlesnakes, as there was certainly not enough dry ground for them. There are many natives, however, who dread the bite of the moccasin quite as much as the rattler, but having seen the fearfully quick work of the latter on several occasions, all known antidotes having been administered in vain, I had occasion to dread it. We encountered very heavy bunches of saw-grass, and the little distance we made to the good was rather disheartening. Hoping to get more easting on the following day, I began looking for a camp. The prospects were more discouraging than the day before. All large islands had disappeared, and nothing was left but small detached groups of bushes, which gave little encouragement even to examine for land.

So we travelled on till it was nearly night, and halted at a little wet island, intending to use it as best we could. There was a knob of land about two inches out of water and four feet in diameter (rather close quarters for two men); this we helped out by throwing down small branches and, finally, fern-leaves, with the tent-fly spread to keep off the dew. After a good supper of fried blue heron and cormorant egg omelet, I finished my note-book work, and we turned in. The camp at Station No. 3 was certainly not a very comfortable one, though I did not wake once during the night, in spite of the racket of frogs, limpkins, etc. I found that the best work could be done in the early morning, so I made a practice of waking up about four o'clock, which gave us good time to finish our breakfast and load the canoes, usually starting just as the sun was rising. That morning proved no exception to our early habits, and everything pointed towards making a good run, but our expectations were far from being realized. Our course seemed completely blocked to the northeast, with nothing but heavy saw-grass, into which every water-lead headed up, and nothing beyond that could be travelled through,—our hardest day's work, and the most discouraging. This central mass of saw-grass no doubt reaches from the south end of Okeechobee to our present latitude, which is 25° 36″ N. Mr. Ingraham crossed it at lat. 26° 10″ N. in his almost fatal attempt to travel in a straight line, having penetrated it so far that the return to Fort Shackelford would be as fruitful of danger as to push on to Miami.

That there is a break somewhere about lat. 25° 50″ known only to the Indians I have little doubt, else how could they travel from the edge of the Big Cypress to Miami with such rapidity. In many places we forced our way through where there was a slight indication of lower grass beyond, but at a terrible expense of muscular power, and the grass cut our hands and faces severely. The day was very hot, and if Everglade water was unwholesome it had a good chance on this occasion to make us ill, for we never limited ourselves in its use.

The only way this hard poling affected me was in causing great pain between my shoulder-blades, which became almost unbearable. Every little while I had to change the object taken for a bearing, when nearly reaching it. It was getting late in the afternoon, and nothing had been accomplished and no place in sight on which to pass the night. Reluctantly we called this a lost day, and headed the canoes on the back trail to Station No. 3, which, by my reverse bearings and the many long stretches already broken through, was not very difficult. After the fight we had made for nothing and the exhausted condition we were in, Station No. 3, that had seemed to us such a miserable place and little better than a make-shift, suddenly became to our minds the cosiest of camps. We cut out more of the bushes, and arranged the tent in connection with the fly so that it made a huge umbrella, and increased the ground space by building up with branches. A few small sweet-bay-trees were standing near us. I cut off the twigs and leaves to make my bed more comfortable than it was the previous night. It reminded me of the beds we used to make of balsam in the Adirondacks, but the smell of the bay is, if anything, more agreeable.

The Indians use the leaves of the sweet-bay also for making a tea which they consider very wholesome. Brewer suggested that we use the inner bark, and, as I had a little extra time for cooking, I made a gallon of this tea, which I poured into my rubber water-bag, to drink cold during the warm work of the day. While I was at work, Brewer took his canoe and said he would make a run to the north and leave an otter-trap a quarter of a mile from us, to be picked up the next day. I hoped for his success, for we had had no meat for some time, and, having used a beaver for the table on one occasion in the Maine woods, I thought perhaps the flesh of the otter (which is similar in its habits) might be as palatable. The character of the Glades had changed but little, the horizon being sharper and fewer clumps of bushes in sight.

From the most easterly point reached on this day I sighted the edge of Long Key and got a bearing to it. The existence of this large island at the southern end of the Everglades has been guessed at by white men, who have seen it from the edge of the pine-timber bordering the Atlantic coast ; but there is no accurate knowledge of its dimensions, and many have vainly tried to reach it. Brewer on one of his hunting expeditions, a few years ago, succeeded in making a landing on the south end, and later in this expedition I crossed the broken part of the north end. Brewer returned at sundown and reported that he had found a lead to the northwest that gave a prospect of getting out in that direction.

The work of the day had told badly on my rubber hip-boots and several cuts had gone through ; these I patched up neatly with my bicycle repair outfit. The bicycle wheel and cyclometer gave most excellent results as a "log." My sights at noon had been carefully worked out and we knew where we were. I could put the point down on the chart; but the question I should have best liked answered then was, Where we shall be to-morrow night? We had gained nothing all day. We awoke next morning having had a most comfortable sleep and feeling in good spirits to encounter whatever difficulties and trials the day might bring forth.

When the sun just began to peep over the horizon it found us in our loaded canoes with pole in hand. We followed the trail that Brewer had broken out the evening before, and made a halt for our otter-trap. Sad to relate, though there were fresh signs all around it, nothing had been caught. After proceeding a mile from Station No. 3, we found a very good lead, which, though carrying us rather more to the north than we wished to go, we followed. It left the worst saw-grass on our right, but by getting farther to the northward we hoped to discover some breaks in this terrible barrier, that seemed to block our northeast course. Though we had seen little game of late, we started three deer, that went plunging through the saw-grass. When I first heard them I picked up my rifle, thinking that some huge animal was about to charge on us, but I soon recognized and located the sound, although they managed to keep entirely out of sight. How with their sharp feet they can get through this grass at all is a mystery, and they must cut their noses frightfully. These deer may have wandered from the western side of the Everglades, though what they can find to feed upon and where they sleep is somewhat of a puzzle.

About eleven o'clock I sighted an island a little to the left of our course, and by a careful examination with the glass I could plainly make out a cabbage-palm growing from its centre. Now, in any other part of Florida the appearance of a cabbage-palm would excite but little interest, as in some places you can see forests of many thousands, but here away out in the Everglades it told a story that gladdened our hearts. It meant dry land. I stopped here to take my usual noon sights, and, though we had made but four miles, we decided to camp on that island. I was sorry that the island could not be reached before the sun crossed the meridian, but did very well without land for my artificial horizon, so after all it made little difference.

I constructed my support in the usual manner by driving three paddles through a few inches of mud to the hard rock bottom, and on the tripod so formed inverting a box to obtain a level surface. This was quite as steady as could be desired. On this I placed my black mirror and levelled it. After carefully noting the vernier reading on the sextant and the time by the two chronometers, I set my " hack watch" and shaped our course for the island. On a nearer approach a dark gap in the trees was seen, and through it a large clearing and plenty of good high ground. At once we saw that we had struck a permanent camp and a very old one, too. I jumped ashore at the canoe landing and found the island deserted; but the many objects of interest around incited me to work at once. The island is nearly circular in shape, supporting a heavy growth of timber, matted together near the ground by thick vines. Near the centre, and approached by a cut-out trail from the eastward, was a clearing about sixty feet in diameter, and like a great tent-pole supporting the canopy of foliage overhead stands the cabbage-palm, whose top projects a few feet above the surrounding trees and had attracted my attention from the distance. On its trunk a few feet above the ground was a smooth place made with a knife; on this a charcoal drawing of a deer's head and body; at one side a double oval somewhat like an elongated figure of eight; beneath and to the right was a figure evidently intended for a squaw; on the left was a hand turned downward. All this is intended to convey some information from one Indian to another. I could not venture upon an interpretation until I should meet some of my Indian friends and describe the place, when, finding that I had visited it, they might be willing to tell me what it signifies.

A hundred years ago there were two other cabbage-palmettos growing on this island, which were larger than the central one. I say a hundred, though it may be many more years than this; the fallen trunks were so rotten that merely a shell remained, and in the position I found them a palmetto would keep sound for a very long time. These trees had not fallen by accident, but were cut down when the clearing was made. Over the ground were strewn a dozen shells of the Everglade terrapin, some probably killed a year ago, others almost reduced to dust, showing great age. It is a custom with the Indians to cook this turtle by broiling it before the fire without removing it from the shell. The flesh is really very good and makes quite a savory stew, resembling when carefully prepared the smaller terrapin that bring such high prices in the Northern market. There were many poles scattered about that had been used for shelters and frames for palmetto " shacks." At one side of the clearing was a place where the cooking-fire had always been made, and over a large pile of ashes were the charred remains of the last pieces of wood that were used.

Now, the Seminole has his own peculiar way of making a fire, as with all Indians his aim is to do the greatest amount of cooking with the least expenditure of wood, prepared with the fewest number of cuts. Though the fire is small, it requires a circular hearth of about sixteen feet in diameter. The wood is cut in six- or eight-feet lengths and placed radially like a huge cart-wheel, a few light twigs starting the fire at the hub. An Indian is constantly moving around the rim of this wheel and pushing the spokes towards the central point an inch or two at a time. A pot is hung from a couple of uprights, or a frying-pan is used in the hand.

The only thing for which I have ever seen them use a frying-pan is for parching their coffee or the making of a kind of pancake.

Their great dependence is "sofkee," which is made in the pot and helped out with a large carved wooden spoon, which is their one article of table or, rather, pot ware, all eating from the same spoon whenever appetite impels them. The best description I can give of "sofkee" is to say that it is the analogue of the Spanish "olla podrida." On the east side of the island stands a sweet-bay-tree, with a crooked trunk, that seemed to invite an easy climb, so before the light waned I took the telescope and without difficulty reached the topmost branch. Looking carefully at the limbs on which I stood, I found that I had not been the first to climb that tree by many. This must have been a favorite place during the Seminole War to keep a lookout constantly posted, to ascertain if any troops had succeeded in passing the natural barriers nature had given to them for protection.

My elevation gave me a marvellous view in every direction, and, by using a powerful aluminum glass, I could distinctly make out the line of timber on the east edge of the Glades, and towards the west the timber-line of the Big Cypress. The distance to each seemed to be about the same. We were in almost the exact centre of the Everglades east and west. No wonder this has been a favorite camping-place of the Seminole, and how many anxious warriors must have climbed this tree and watched from this very perch for long hours during the war, and with what joy they greeted the news from the North that no further attempt would be made to conquer them, a verbal agreement having been entered upon that so long as they let the white settlers alone no further steps would be taken against them. The vicinity of this spot had been one of my objective-points, as it was near the centre of an unknown area, bounded on the north by the two previous lines of exploration, and much to the south of the line made by scouting parties of troops. I felt for once in my life that I had reached ground never before touched by a white man, and in my enthusiasm took my little New York Yacht Club flag from my pocket and Brewer christened the island Willoughby Key.

After remaining for some time in the tree-top, I joined Brewer on the ground and communicated to him the result of my observations. What most interested him was the finding of good water-leads to the eastward; but on this point I could give him little encouragement. It is rather a strange thing that from a great elevation you are much disappointed at the amount of water seen; in fact, you see no water at all, nothing but grass, and as for doing advance piloting, you might just as well be standing in your canoe. I made up my mind that in the future, if opportunity presented, to climb no more trees with this purpose in view. This is the first camp in which we were really comfortable. The tent was pitched to its full proportions, with the fly extending over the front.

On the remains of the Indian fire we built up a most cheerful blaze, as there was an abundance of dry wood about, and in a very short time I notified Brewer that supper was ready. Our supper on this occasion was very much as usual, but the hot embers enabled me to broil a limpkin, which gave a pleasant change from the frying-pan. The camp was so picturesque that before sunset I made an attempt to get a picture with the camera, but the light was so weak that I feared poor results, the clearing being obscured by heavy foliage. This has been my difficulty with nearly all the choicest bits worth preserving. During the run of the day Brewer was so unfortunate as to break a pole, which had jammed in a crevice in the rock, and he would have been in a very bad fix to replace it had I not insisted at starting upon carrying an extra one. The shelter-poles the Indians have left here were all too crooked for the purpose of poling.

CHAPTER VI

E made our usual morning start after
breakfast. My object was to take
bearings that would lead me to the
east and find, by zigzagging the leads, a route
to get through this impenetrable barrier of saw-
grass. This day was one of our hardest, and
yet we made the least number of miles, only
gaining two miles and a half to the eastward.
Fifty times or more, leads that seemed good
headed up in saw-grass that was nine or ten
feet high, with hardly any water at its roots. I
was tempted to strike a due east course, but the
rate of travel would immediately be reduced to
a mile a day, and should the strip prove to be
fifteen miles across, the chances of starvation
would be great.

This part of the Everglades seems to be devoid of animal and bird life; a few small black
bass are occasionally seen near deeper holes in

the rock bottom, but we would have had to devote the greater part of the day to catching them. We had about three pounds of bacon left, and, as it was important in frying, also to use as butter, if that gave out, we would feel its loss greatly. Our last pieces of ham and cheese had been consumed, but we still had a few pounds of dry crawfish and some potatoes in the bag. I had no fear of the groceries and portable food giving out. We had not used half of it yet, and the supply of cocoa was not one-third exhausted. The poling was most trying on my shoulders, and at times the pain would be so great that I would be afraid to sit down in the canoe, lest I should get so stiff that I could not continue before a proper day's work had been accomplished. Probably the mental annoyance had much to do with my fatigue. Even Brewer, accustomed as he was to this arduous poling, acknowledged, for the first time, that he was completely " played out."

Still we fought on, and about five o'clock in the afternoon a small clump of bushes was reached, and we made camp at Station No. 5 as best we could. After clearing out these bushes there was barely room to stretch our cheese-cloths; the ground was very soft and wet, a great contrast to the dry island we were on the night before. The kerosene-stove was a great comfort here, as I soon had a good hot supper ready, and, though I felt sore all over, I managed to do my usual plotting and navigating before I put the lantern out to retire to my uncomfortable couch, which was but an inch above the water; but for the rubber blankets we would have been thoroughly wet through before morning; as it was, only the lower end of my sleeping-bag was slightly damp.

I have not said very much about snakes, but it must not be supposed that these agreeable creatures were absent; the very places we selected for camps were usually the ones appreciated by their snakeships, and the first careful work we usually did was to clear them out before trusting our legs too recklessly in dark corners. There are many varieties that live in the Everglades, and their numbers have certainly not been exaggerated by other explorers. Our start on the following day was not quite as early as usual, as Brewer and I were somewhat muscle-sore by our unusually tiresome work of the day before. We managed to get under way an hour after sunrise, but before poling very far in the cool air we felt that we were equal to the day's possible trials and vexations. We first started to the east, and could make no headway at all, the saw-grass in this direction being even heavier than we had yet seen it, and not an opening could be discovered. We abandoned an easterly course after several hours, but what made things more serious was that our further progress to the north was also blocked. From this point I could see an Indian ring-fire due north about forty miles distant, well up towards Okeechobee, probably made by some of the Micasukees. To the west was a similar ring-fire on the edge of the Big Cypress Swamp. The latter I could easily account for as being about the position where my friends Robert Osceola, Little Tiger, Johnnie Billie, and Dr. Jimmie were having their big otter-hunt. To the eastward I could see a column of smoke that was not of Indian origin. It was in the exact bearing that the Miami River should be, and, after making a careful examination through the glass, both Brewer and myself decided that it came from the mill or a steamboat at the mouth of the river.

Across the Everglades

Miami seemed so near, and yet, as the sequence proved, how many miles we were destined to travel before reaching it! It seemed hard, after making so much easting, that we could not get by that terrible strip of grass, into which I did not dare venture, and to penetrate even but a short distance might take weeks of most trying labor and, what was worse, exhaust our supply of provisions. I weighed the matter very carefully, and determined that the longest way round was the shortest way through. The character of the Everglades at this point was similar to what it had been for the past two days. The water was still clear and running at the rate of from half a mile to a mile an hour in a southwesterly direction, at times showing a symptom of moving southerly even a little east of south. This showed me clearly that we were very near the dividing water-shed which runs down the centre of the State and has its terminus in the heart of the Everglades. The rock is everywhere found, usually smooth, in very many places with no mud on top of it. Where it underlies the big saw-grass it is occasionally seven or eight feet under. But the coralline limestone can always be depended on as not being very far off.

Across the Everglades

Crevices in the rock were still passed, but I could not stop to ascertain about how much water was coming directly from this source. Before making camp for the night I had come to the conclusion that there was but one safe course opened to us, and that was to travel on our back trail till the first opening to the eastward presented itself, and then make our northing good again, coming up on the eastern edge of the long tongue of saw-grass. There was a ray of comfort in our disappointments, and that was that I had reached a central point upon which before starting I had put my pencil and said to Brewer, " That is the locality that I am most anxious to reach, for many people suppose large islands may there be found ;" and as not to find them proved one of my theories, I was less annoyed at the partial retracing of our steps.

The canoes were beginning to show the effects of the terrible rubbing and scraping to which they had been subjected. The paint and varnish were nearly all worn off the bottoms, and they would not run much farther without another coat, but a whole day could not be spared for this work. Our camp was much the counterpart of the one of last night, if anything the patch of ground was smaller and had to be pieced out with sticks and leaves. Nothing but the fly of the tent could be used as a shelter.

As Station No. 6 was a very important one, I took more time than usual to work out my sights at noon, and was much pleased to find that my various ways of obtaining distance corresponded closely, and I felt that the plotting on my chart was so far accurate. The almost perpetual sunshine was varied to-day by many clouds, and I was greatly in hopes that during the night we would get a good rain. I could see by the water-line on the grass that it was lowering at the rate of a quarter of an inch a day, which gave me uneasiness. The work was certainly hard enough as it was, but with less water and the dry season coming on, the future looked dark enough. Nothing could be killed to add to our provisions, our last piece of bacon had disappeared, and but one dried crawfish remained. We had seen two Everglade terrapin during the day, but were not able to capture them. Only an occasional fish was seen, and small ones at that, hardly large enough to warrant the expenditure of many hours in their capture.

Making an early start from Station No. 6, we poled south, and by my reverse bearings, and the fresh trail to help us, we made rapid progress. Before the sun had crossed the meridian we were at Station No. 5, a day's work completed in half a day. This was made possible by having so few detours and the boats slipping with greater ease through the old trail. The usual noonday halt of an hour was made for dinner and rest, after which we continued on the back trail, watching the country continually to the eastward to discover any gaps that offered sufficient inducements to penetrate for any distance; but, as on our outward journey, there seemed to be no possibility of getting to the eastward.

On the bottom, near a smooth rocky surface, I saw what I took to be a dead fish, which I stopped and picked up, and, much to my surprise, found it to be something that looked like a fish with a tail at each end. On a closer examination it proved to be two large-mouthed black bass, each ten inches in length. One had attempted to swallow the other, resulting in the death of both. This singular duel could not have occurred many hours before, as the flesh was quite fresh, though the doubt as to the time that had elapsed since their death forbade our using them in the frying-pan. The food for fish must be scarce in this section when small fish of this size have taken to eating up each other. Early in the afternoon we sighted Willoughby Key, and made directly for it. After the uncomfortable camps we had made recently, it was like getting home.

My attention was at once arrested by the appearance of the old camp-fire. The ashes and charred wood were scattered in every direction. Surely some one had been there since we left the spot. Who could it have been? On closer examination, Brewer and myself decided that nothing could have left this sign but otter; there seemed to have been six or eight of them, and the dry ashes had apparently offered a means of getting rid of the insects on them, or of drying their fur. They had evidently run up to the fireplace, then gone to the nearest tree-trunk, rubbed and rolled, repeating the process several times. A little to one side of the cabbage-palm were the freshly scattered feathers of a large bird, the body of which had been eaten, leaving but few bones. This did not look like the work of otter, and after examining the soft mould we found the fresh track of a panther. We thought perhaps his catship might return again, finding no other dry place on which to sleep if still in the vicinity; but he probably smelled our fire, and we got no chance for a shot.

Still a little time remained before sunset, which we devoted to making camp and taking an observation from the Indian watch-tower in the tree-top. The tent was fully set up on a smooth piece of ground, with the fly extended to the front nearly to the fire, and plenty of wood was cut and a good blaze started. A large kettle of sweet-bay tea was prepared to drink cold when travelling. While unloading the canoes, standing in the water with my hip-boots on, my working compass dropped from its lanyard and settled in the soft mud. I did not dare to move, but, stooping gently, I began groping around in the direction it had disappeared, and by great good luck soon recovered it. Being nearly water-tight, it was soon put in order. We would have felt the loss of this compass very much, as it was so convenient for the short bearings, being a most accurate instrument and an old companion on land and sea for twenty years, the larger asimuth compass taking more time to manipulate. Our camp that night was by far the most comfortable of any we had made, and looked more like a permanent one than if intended for " one night only."

Across the Everglades

As my navigation and chart work was somewhat simplified on returning to a known station, I was enabled to retire much earlier than usual, dropping off into such a deep sleep that Brewer could hardly wake me up at our usual hour for turning out. Nothing short of a rattlesnake crawling over my legs and sounding his castanets could have disturbed me. The extra room for moving about this camp and the comparatively soft beds we had used made us feel quite strong and fresh for the continuance of our journey.

When breakfast was over and everything packed, we branched off from our old trail and kept a more southerly course, the trend of the water enabling us to do this, and the slight current was in our favor. A northerly wind was also blowing, which made poling much easier than usual, except when the leads headed up and we would have to back out of them. Many times during the day we tried to gain more easting, but without success. Should we have to go clear to the sea before getting around the south end of that terrible saw-grass? I was aware that on the west the Shark River was the last place by which the coast could be reached by a human being with a canoe, and on the east things were nearly as bad, the first stream

emerging from that side being the **Miami River.**
The feeling that we were boxed up in this manner was not a very pleasant one ; but we declared
that, as we had set out to make **Miami** through
the Everglades, no obstacle should be permitted
to baffle us in our undertaking.

Progress might at times be slow, but with
the exception of the one day we were obliged
to go nearly in a circle, returning to our starting-point, we had always made at least three
miles for the day's work, and, as we had plenty
of groceries left, the fear of starving did not
trouble us very much, though we felt the
need of fresh meat. The diet of a vegetarian
never seemed to me suitable for hard work. I
never felt better in my life, but was conscious
of losing somewhat in flesh. We were making
rapid progress, but unless we were able to make
at least ten miles of our surround-work, we felt
it would almost be better to tackle the big saw-
grass at the rate of half a mile a day.

I got a shot at a limpkin, which I missed,
probably, in my anxiety not to let him escape,
requiring too much from the range of the gun.
So our dinner took unto itself wings, and we
were not even able to catch a turtle. The
game, however, promises to become plentiful.

Across the Everglades

It was past our usual time for camping before we sighted an island that gave any promise of a dry spot. On starting in to cut out bushes, I found that several deer had been there the night before. On a little circle about six feet in diameter a buck and two does had made a snug little nest. The ferns had been pressed down smoothly by their bodies, showing plainly the outlines of their forms. As compared with islands upon which we have camped, this little spot, elevated but a few inches above the water, seemed perfection, though there was hardly enough room to set the tent in its full shape. The deer had evidently made a comfortable night here, and we hoped to be as fortunate.

The next day was Sunday, the 17th of January, and as we had been travelling so continuously (last Sunday there being no place to stop), we were beginning to feel the need of a day of rest and an opportunity to dry and repair the bottoms of the canoes. My surveying work had been rather easier, as, looking towards the south, I could get objects of more distinct shape, but when once decided on an object and figured up to it, I had never mistaken it, as both Brewer and I kept it constantly before our eyes, and the indentations on the horizon were not many. If we never got a worse camp than that at Station No. 8, that the deer had chosen for us, we would have great reason to be thankful.

What a delightful feeling of rest it was, after getting awake at four o'clock the next morning, to drop off to sleep again and know nothing till the sun was quite high in the sky, and then lie still for another hour, until the feeling of hunger reminded us that a hot bowl of oatmeal and a cup of as good coffee as could be procured at Delmonico's would be just the "lacking ingredient" at this time! There was still no sign of rain. The water was getting each day lower; our big detours had made it necessary to consume more time and provisions than we had expected. We had started for the Miami, and to the Miami we were bound. to go, at the same time taking up our explorations as near east to Station No. 6 as the width of that terrible strip of saw-grass would permit. We had been baffled, but not conquered. The superb pluck of Brewer always dissipated any latent misgivings in my own mind as to the ultimate result of our undertaking. Our health was good, no accident had occurred, and

I could foresee none, with our system and care, unless one of us should be so unfortunate as to be bitten by the snakes that so abounded.

After making a few courses to the southward, we at last found signs that we had reached the south end of the line of big sawgrass. The rock was more frequently near the surface, and could not support the heavier growth, but as one obstacle grew less another became greater. The water was lower and bore the canoes with great difficulty. The progress, too, was very slow, and much wading had to be done, easing the canoes over bad places as much as possible. Take it altogether, this more open travel was to be preferred, though more trying to the legs, than the hard pushing through the high, cutting grass. Occasionally a good water-lead would help us on our way, and we were at last headed to the northeast.

But with all our work the amount of easting did not exceed a mile and a half, as it had only been on the last two courses that we made anything in that direction. That afternoon I killed a blue heron and a limpkin, which was an acquisition to our larder, especially as the limpkin was young and tender. There seemed to be the same difficulty that we had met all along in selecting a good place for a camp and to establish Station No. 9. But at last a little island hove in sight with large enough bushes on it to invite an investigation. Brewer waded ashore and said he thought it might do, and as it was getting late we made camp.

The island was surrounded with saw-grass, and we made a trail to it by running a canoe through several times, which required much extra exertion. With axe and brush-hook we soon had it cleared, and found about the usual amount of wet ground,—some twenty square yards. It was hard on these small patches to find a place where the canoes could be turned bottom up to dry and examine. I have adopted a method of throwing them on top of the saw-grass, which is so strong that it keeps them a couple of feet out of the water. Unloading the canoes after the arduous work of the day on the places we were forced to camp seemed like a waste of strength, and was much like wasted work. In my conceit as an old camper I had made an error in selecting my canoes for this journey. I expected always to find dry islands ; such were conspicuous by their absence. The Seminole when travelling always sleeps in his boat, but not until many nights spent on wet ground did I realize why this was necessary. The canoe which I proposed to use for my intended hunting-trip the next winter would be seventeen feet long and twenty-eight inches beam, weighing about one hundred pounds, built of cedar, with heavy bilge keels; otherwise, the Canadian model.

I have not tried steel canoes, but as it would insure a tight boat and would drag well, it might be a good material with which to build. A repair like a puncture could be made with solder. The dimensions given above would insure easy poling, and at night the load could be placed in each end, giving plenty of space to sleep. A canoe shelter, with cheese-cloth inside, similar to those used on the old Shadow canoe, or the Indian method of driving four stakes outside of the boat to support the cheese-cloth, would afford greater comfort. After starting supper on the kerosene-stove and sitting down on one of the camp-chests, I happened to look down towards the canoes through the little tunnel of foliage we had made, and on a limb, within two feet of where our heads had passed many times in our trips with the canoe loads, was a five-foot snake. He had been watching us all this time, and kept his wicked little eyes on our every movement.

I now took my turn at watching him for a time, to see if he would move when he found himself observed. But no ; he had evidently made his camp also for the night, with no intention whatever of allowing any one to disturb him. So I picked up the shot-gun and gave him a load of small shot in order not to spoil his skin. He dropped from the limb, but was caught in a crotch and wedged near his tail, so that he hung down nearly his full length, with blood running from where the shot had gone into his backbone, as dead as snakes usually are inside of twelve hours.

We continued our supper, giving no further thought to the reptile, as snakes had by this time become a familiar sight. After finishing my evening task on my map and notes, and the important operation of winding my chronometers, I disappeared under my cheese-cloth. but somehow could not go to sleep as usual, Looking out towards the open Glades, I saw, silhouetted against the bright moonlight, that miserable snake, which I had forgotten all about, his body assuming those easy curves that snakes only can make. I rolled over on my other side, but my eyes kept getting back to that snake, and I soon found that sleep would be impossible so long as it hung there. Brewer was snoring in such bliss that I had not the heart to disturb him, so I turned out and with the help of a short stick pulled the reptile from the branch.

The mosquitoes, that had not been troublesome in most of our camps, were abundant here, and I dreaded lest some of them would follow me under the net, and they did. But after that ghastly picture had been destroyed, I had no trouble in going to sleep in spite of them. The day had been most fatiguing, the water being so low and the rock getting rougher. Just before reaching Station No. 9 we had sighted Long Key, but we were too far to the north to see anything of the royal palm-trees.

On the 19th of January we were under way at seven o'clock, and the weather being cooler made us feel like putting a good stretch of country behind us. We had not proceeded far before Brewer broke the foot of his only pole. As the bottom was all rock here, the accident would not cause any delay, so I tossed him a spare foot which I carried in my canoe, telling him to put it on in camp that evening. The islands were becoming more frequent, and on many of them there were, no doubt, patches of ground, but we pushed on as long as we could see islands ahead that seemed dry. For the first time since leaving Willoughby Key we saw a cabbage-palm, which was a very encouraging sight, as it meant more dry ground. Our noonday meal was rather an unsatisfactory one of cold boiled potatoes. Our biscuit had given out, and I had to try my hand at bread-making over the stove during the evening. A few better leads were met with the next day, but the water was provokingly shoal, more rock showing itself, over which the grass grew thinly. Long Key lay to the east; the timber on it could be seen occasionally. A very interesting landmark for which I had been steering was a tall pine-tree on a small island. I say interesting, for it was such an uncommon sight to us, and meant not only dry land, but very dry land. This tree had been in sight since the day before, and that afternoon we were leaving it well astern. Our distance on that day was eight and a half miles, though the log showed nearly fifteen, but in the Everglades this must be regarded as a pretty straight course.

The islands were getting closer together, and by three o'clock we made camp on one which seemed especially adapted to our purposes. The

water ran close up to it, and from its centre
grew two cabbage-palms. After the usual clearing was made I cut down one of the cabbage-
palms and extracted the cabbage, to form a
relish for our evening meal. Very few people,
even in Florida, know how delicious the cabbage from the palm can be made. The simplest
way is to cut it up raw and use it as cold-slaw;
it is tender and has a slight nutty flavor. Boiled
as ordinary cabbage, it is excellent. In addition
to cabbage, this variety of palm bears a black
berry about the size of a pea, which resembles
a little in flavor the Chinese litchi nut, but the
seed is so large in proportion to the nut that
many have to be gathered to get much out of
them. The heart of the scrub-palmetto can
also be used as is the cabbage-palm, but many
have to be cut and prepared to afford a dish.
This camp was by far the best we had made
since the one on Willoughby Key, the ground
being dry and the water coming well up to the
shore, making a short carry for the canoe loads.
To the east many islands can be seen, and a
line of timber, which is on the west edge of
Long Key. Station No. 10 was established,
and the camp was a most satisfactory one.

CHAPTER VII

Canoeing over Two Inches of Water—Nearing the End—
Welcome to Civilization—Analysis of Water—Seminole
Vocabulary.

THE following day we attempted to run on a northeast course, but the water was so low that after many fruitless efforts we decided that we must get more to the eastward, and then followed one of the most exhausting and trying days experienced yet, in which we were out of our canoes nearly all the time ; poling was impossible, and dragging for hours became a necessity. It seemed the choice of evils between the big saw-grass country or the section we were then in. Plenty of small high islands surrounded us, and the water about them was so shoal that a loaded canoe could not be floated. The bare rock was everywhere visible, with hardly any grass. This rock had entirely lost its smooth character, and was very rough, little peaks sticking out of the water like stalagmites in a cave, and, though of soft coralline limestone, had very sharp edges and corners, which cut the bottoms of the canoes in a terrible way, so that both boats were leaking badly. Things became serious, the best method to advance more puzzling. Poling was impossible, and portages could not be made, no wading, with a load on the back, could be thought of, as there were thousands of deep holes among the rocks, in which the legs would jam, with imminent danger of fracture.

It was not safe to leave the bow or stern of the boats, dependent as we were on their friendly support. Every now and then the canoes would get wedged in the rocks, taking several minutes to extricate them. The advance could be counted by inches, as the halts had to be made every few hundred feet in order to bail the canoes. The sun was hot and the wind light, so that the perspiration trickled in a stream down our backs, and the amount of water we drank was something surprising. Surely this Everglade water must be a wholesome beverage, for we gave it a thorough trial that day. All these islands are really the broken part of Long Key; they become fewer and fewer to the north, extending in all about three miles. Towards the south the islands become thicker and larger till they reach Long Key proper. This was evidently the termination of the ridge of rough rocks that forms the high land of the key itself, and if we could only get three miles to the eastward we would reach better water for the canoes.

We were very tired towards evening. The work of the day had brought into play a somewhat different set of muscles. The difficult wading, the lifting of the feet out of holes in the rock, the pulling, dragging, and the extra care necessary to avoid tearing the loaded canoes to pieces exhausted us terribly. Brewer felt this day's work more than I, and he declared he would rather pole a canoe over dry ground. It was important that we should gain more distance to the eastward, for I had every reason to believe that this dividing ridge could not extend many miles, crossing it as we were at right angles. Amid our troubles and vexations we were certain of a good dry camp for the night.

The islands, though small, were high, many of them having several cabbage-palms upon them, and so close together that very short compass-bearings could alone be taken. At six o'clock we selected an island and prepared to camp. Before doing anything else I repaired the bottom of both canoes with canvas and varnish.

Many cuts were through, the holes causing serious leaks during the day, but I had no doubt that I could make them quite tight again. The shape of the island on which we were camped was circular, rising to about four feet in the centre, at which point grew a tall pine. With the exception of a high island to the east, this was the only one on which pine-wood was growing. We found that even a high island might have its inconveniences, as the land at Station No. 11 was so sloping that in the middle of the night we nearly slid into the water. Continuing an easterly route the next day, we encountered much the same obstacles in the way of rough rock near the surface. At last we cleared the ridge, and the face of the rock began to get smoother, and more of the round grass and deeper water could be seen ahead.

Brewer thought that we would not have many more miles to travel before reaching a district that he had hunted over when going in from the east coast. He had followed down the pine-timber of the main land at a sufficient distance from it to find it insured deep enough water for the canoes. Finding better leads, we were now able to take the much-desired northeasterly direction, and about noon we sighted a small, high island that on approaching Brewer recognized as the one on which he had camped the previous year. He had made a small clearing, and there was plenty of dry wood. This was the first evidence of the previous presence of a white man that we had met since leaving the west coast, and we felt almost as if the difficulties of our journey were at an end; but I wished to get well to the northward before striking east to Miami, and by so doing get as near Station No. 6 as possible, in order that nothing of importance would escape that might lie between this line and the above-mentioned station.

This gave us many miles of travel yet, but we hoped that better water would make poling easier. At this old camp of Brewer's I established Station No. 12, and as game was abundant in this vicinity I hoped to return to it another winter for the purposes of hunting. The canoes needed attention again, as they had been leaking badly during the day. Many deer and birds were seen between Stations Nos.

1 and 12. A large buck stood so long that Brewer tried to shoot at him, but, not being accustomed to my heavy-calibre rifle, the ball failed to hit, to my regret, as our larder was in a condition that justified the killing. Clouds had been gathering all day, but the rain that we so desired never came.

It was then the 22d of January, and, unless the usual order of things failed, we had no right to expect showers before March. The water was certainly getting lower every day, but with our northward course we should find better channels. From Station No. 12 the travel became more rapid; we had left the thickly clustered islands, and the horizon to the north and east was assuming the same lonely, desolate appearance that it had in the central portions. To the east, however, the faint line of pine on the main land could be seen. At noon we reached an Indian camp that had been deserted for some time. Near the landing the skeletons of twelve alligators and two otters had been left after skinning. The heads of the alligators were badly knocked to pieces, the teeth having been removed from the jaws.

Old canoe-trails were leading from this camp

in many directions, and, selecting one that led towards the northeast, we made rapid progress. After almost despairing of finding a camp for the night, we were compelled to make use of the first clump of bushes in sight after four o'clock. Brewer was busy with the bush-hook levelling the small piece of wet ground, when he suddenly gave a cry of alarm. I jumped out of the canoe to ascertain the trouble, and found that a large moccasin had struck at his legs at close quarters, but had missed him. A narrow escape for which we were truly most thankful.

The run for the day had been eleven and one-quarter miles, and the course of the canoes was very much more direct than usual. If as long a run could be made on the following day, the head of the Miami River should be in sight. The canoes again needed repair, Brewer's being in the worst condition. Looking to the westward from Station No. 13, I could see the heavy saw-grass that we had been unable to cross from Station No. 6, and by my map I found that it was seven miles wide. Fifty-five miles around to save those seven miles of big saw-grass, and I did not in the least regret the caution that had dictated this long detour. The canoes had, of course, travelled much farther, as the above distance was measured on the compass courses. I was reconciled to the enforced lengthening of my line of survey, as this huge zigzag had thrown light on a section that would probably have remained in the dark for some time to come.

After a good night's rest we continued our journey, being enabled by the straighter and deeper water-leads to make a better course for the Miami River. Near the middle of the day the country began to look very familiar, and I saw in the distance an island that, from a peculiar-shaped tree that grew on it, I knew at once as being the camp of Miami Jimmie and the Tiger family that I had visited the previous year. At one o'clock we arrived at the camp, but a disappointment awaited me. Hardly a sign to remind me of the old place remained. A white man had taken possession of the island, driving the Indians away, destroying their palmetto shacks, and giving them to understand that the land belonged to the white man.

On the ruins of the picturesque Indian village, that we had so much admired the year before, was built an unsightly wooden shanty, and the quadrangle around which the palmetto shacks had stood was occupied by a rude vegetable garden.

The happy little faces we remembered, the squaws busying themselves with their household cares, the stalwart braves returning laden from the chase, the air of quiet contentment which pervaded the scene, had vanished to return never again. Poor Miami Jimmie so loved the Miami River that he could not tear himself away from its vicinity, and had taken up his abode on a little island five miles distant; the rest had gone to the Big Cypress. This white man had taken advantage of the unwillingness of the Seminole to provoke hostilities. The Indians had gone without a murmur, but through no spirit of cowardice; the blood that fills their veins to-day is as brave as any spilled in the Seminole War, and their courage is as high now as then, but loyalty to their pledge makes them submit to many an outrage. Some day I hope to interest myself in their behalf when an opportunity presents itself.

The island was deserted at the time we arrived, but we met the white settler's man making his way back to the island from Miami in a flat skiff. I was so long without seeing

the face of a human being other than Brewer's
that I thought it would be pleasant to meet
some one. I would have liked to make inqui-
ries in regard to the state of affairs in Cuba, but
to the hireling of so mean a "land-grabber"
my heart did not go out. We were then
moving along at a rapid rate, there being a
well-cut trail leading from the island in a northeasterly direction.

We soon saw ahead the well-known gap in
the cypress-trees on the edge of the Glades at
which the Miami River takes its rise. We felt
that we were really nearing home. Entering
the Miami where it was but a few feet wide, we
were hurried rapidly along, and as it was getting
late and we were very tired, having covered
fifteen miles, we thought it best to camp a
short distance down the river at a place that
has been used by the Seminoles for many
years. The sight of the cypress- and pine-trees
was very restful to our eyes, that had grown
accustomed to looking at nothing higher than
the horizon.

Near our camp was a pretty spring of clear
water that rushed from the side of the hill.
There was plenty of room in the little clearing
to pitch the tent once more to its full propor-

tions and for making a few repairs on the canoes. Here we met some negroes, from whom we obtained fish, which helped out our meagre fare. We also met a sportsman who had been fishing on the upper river. We plied him with so many questions that he must have thought we had just landed from the antipodes, but when I gave him my name he was all interest, and in turn began questioning me. My friends in Miami had, he told me, been waiting anxiously for news ; that the " Cupid," with Sam on board, had been back a week, reporting our starting to the Everglades from the Gulf of Mexico. As he intended reaching Miami that night, I sent several messages by him.

Devoting more time than usual to the map I was making, I was gratified to find that my calculations had brought me to within half a mile of the source of the river. By my diary it should have been Saturday night,—I had made Brewer keep the record of time and the days of the week, and the two tallied. We made a hasty supper, and our beds were so comfortable that it was late the next morning when we awoke. The canoes were loaded for the last time, and we shoved off into the swift current of the river. How beautiful everything seemed on that quiet Sunday morning! No exertion was necessary but the light turn of the paddle to give the canoes their proper course. The four miles seemed like one when we reached the last bend.

A house-boat was moored near the river bank, on which a man sat reading a newspaper, from which he looked up in an inquiring way at our loaded canoes and bronzed faces. A few more strokes and we ran alongside the dock from which we had started a month before. My coming had been already heralded, and there was a little crowd assembled to welcome my return. Foremost among them we saw the smiling face of Sam Roberts, and his first remark after congratulating me upon my success was, " Why, you are going to have a good-shaped nose after all, but you look mighty thin."

And so ends my " Trip across the Everglades."

ANALYSIS OF WATER FROM THE EVERGLADES

100,000 parts contain :

Total solids	31.4 parts.
Silica	0.28 part.
Iron oxide and alumina . .	0.64 part.
Lime	8.48 parts.
Magnesia	trace.
Chlorides	4.65 parts.
Nitrites	none.
Nitrates	none.
Sulphates	none.
Ammonia	none.
Organic matter	trace.

Solid matter, chiefly salt (trace), and calcium carbonate.

VOCABULARY OF THE SEMINOLE LANGUAGE

A.

Accordion	Hi-eets-caw.
Adam's apple	No-quif-pa-tock-ock-naw.
Air-plant	Aw-shen-lock-o.
Alive	Hee-sah-kee.
Alligator	Aal-pa-tah.
Ankle	E-lay-tooke-to-snaw.
Ant (black)	Tock-o-cha-lus-tee.
Ant (red)	Tock-o-cha-cha-tee.
Antlers	E-cho-yi-pee.
Apple	Shot-o-lock-o.
Arm	E-shock-pan.
Arm (left)	Aw-clos-clin-aw.
Arm (left, above elbow)	Aw-kos-ko-nof-o-nee.
Arm (right)	In-clop-pe-claw.
Arm (right, above elbow)	Sock-pof-o-nee.
Armpits	Ho-lo-wa-to-tee-ta-gaw.
Arrow	Chot-a-dox-cha-in-chee.
Ashes	Tock-ees-so.
Awl	Shif-fon-wah.
Axe	Pa-chas-wah.

B.

Bachelor	E-hi-was-ko.
Back	E-claw.
Backbone	E-claw-fo-nee.
Back of hand	In-tee-ta-pix-tee-e-naw-pa.
Back teeth	E-no-tee-lock-ko.
Bad	Holwa-gus.
Banana	We-len-tee-lo.

168

Across the Everglades

Barefoot	Es-tel-e-pi-e-ca-och-a-co.
Bare head	Cop-a-to-ca-och-a-co.
Basket	Som-pa-chee.
Beads	Co-na-waw.
Bear	Lo-ko-see.
Beard	No-ti-ka-is-see.
Bear-skin (robe)	Lo-cus-haft-ee-pa-ta-ko.
Beaver-skin	O-sho-aw-haft-bee.
Bed	Pa-tan-can.
Bee (drone)	Chil-lock-o-fa.
Beetle (black)	Soxe-so.
Bell	Chum-chan-cho-lock-ke.
Bird	Fuss-wah.
Biscuit	Tol-a-la-go-chee.
Black	Luss-tee.
Blackberry	Gatch-ho-ho-e-claw.
Blackbird	O-chot-aw.
Blackbird (red wing)	Shock-kit-law.
Black-snake	Chit-ta-lus-tee.
Bladder	E-ho-sit-waw.
Blanket	Ech-e-taw.
Blaze	Lits-la-it.
Blood	Chaw-taw.
Blue	Ok-ho-la-tee.
Boat	Pah-lo.
Body	E-naw-chee.
Bog	On-lee-wah-nee.
Bone (cow)	Wa-ka-e-fo-nee.
Boy	Che-pon-no.
Brain (man)	E-kol-pee.
Brass	Chat-o-lon-ee.
Bread	Tock-a-la-kee.
Bread (corn)	O-chee-tot-o-la-go-chee.
Breast (man)	E-hoke-pee.
Breast (woman)	E-pee-see.
Breech-cloth	E-kof-kaw.
Breech-cloth-belt	She-won-nock-e-taw.
Brick	Tock-kin-o-shaw.

Seminole Vocabulary

Broom	Sin-ti-ne-ta-pi-ee-te-caw.
Broomstick	Op-pee.
Brother	E-chock-a-tee.
Brother (older)	E-la-ha.
Brother (younger)	E-cho-see.
Brown	Ho-ko-lon-i-tee.
Brush	Tol-lot-to-chee.
Bucket	Sto-caw.
Buckskin	Cho-see.
Buggy	Tost-to-lese-ta-pof-no-chee.
Burn	No-clit.
Butter	Wa-ka-pish-a-ne-haw.

C.

Cactus	Gout-lock-o.
Cake	Tot-o-lo-som-po-chee.
Cake (small)	Tock-a-la-kee-chum-po-chee.
Calf	Wal-ka-chee.
Calf (of leg)	E-lim-pock-ko.
Canoe	Bith-low.
Cap	Cot-to-po-kaw.
Cartridge	Chat-o-ko-cho.
Cat	Po-sha-chee.
Cat (wild)	Ko-wat-go-chee.
Catfish	Sar-sho-o-kee-lon-waw.
Cauliflower	Ist-so-lock-ko.
Chair	O-like-a-taw.
Chameleon	Kon-kla-po-chee.
Cheek	E-yan-i-waw.
Cheese	Wa-ka-pish-aw-lock-o-la-kee.
Cherries	Pe-kon-o-soch-o-chee.
Chewing-gum	Hil-o-cho-waw.
Chicken	To-to-lo-chee.
Chicken (Mother Carey's)	E-chee-pa-hot-tee.
Chief	Micco-or-lee-a-pati-ya.
Child	Es-to-chee.
Chin	No-ti-caw.

Across the Everglades

Chip . . . . Ech-to-fa-la-ho-lee.
Clock . . . . Ach-a-kil-caw-lock-o.
Cloud . . . . Ho-lo-chee.
Coat . . . . Ai-o-kof-kee-lah.
Cocoanut . . . . Tol-o-so-caw.
Colt . . . . Chil-lock-o-chee.
Comb . . . . Ees-cos-caw.
Compass, To . . . . Aw-lock-chay.
Compass . . . . E-skil-caw.
Cord-wood . . . . To-fo-la-hi-lee.
Corn . . . . Chee.
Corn-bread . . . . O-chee-tot-o-la-go-chee.
Corn (green) . . . . Och-chee-lo-wat-kee.
Cow . . . . Wal-ka.
Creek . . . . Hatch-o-o-chee.
Crow . . . . O-shaw-o-waw.
Cry (to) . . . . Hock-ka-eet-kit.
Cup . . . . Hi-lo-chee.
Curlew . . . . Hi-lo-lo.
Curlew (pink) . . . . . . Hi-lo-lo-chaw-tee.

D.

Dark . . . . Um-us-ka-taw.
Date (to) . . . . E-lo-chaw.
Day . . . . Nit-taw.
Day (To-) . . . . Mon-son-nit-taw.
Dead . . . . E-lot-tee.
Death . . . . Il-lit.
Deer-meat . . . . E-cho-push-waw.
Deer-skin (robe) . . . . . E-cho-haft-ee-pa-ta-kaw.
Deer-walk . . . . E-cho-yak-op-po-sit.
Dew . . . . Chit-cho.
Dog . . . . E-faw.
Door . . . . Shot-ho-te-caw.
Doorway . . . . Aw-ho-gee.
Dove . . . . Posh-e-ho-we.
Duck . . . . Fo-cho.

Seminole Vocabulary

E.

Eagle	Hat-tit-e-fon-caw.
Ear	E-hots-ko.
Ear-lobe	Hots-cote-es-caw.
East	Ha-so-saw.
East star	Ho-so-shaw.
Egg	Its-hoos-tas-gay.
Elbow	E-poo-chee.
Enemy	Ho-thlee.
Entrails	Fit-chee-law-pots-kee.
Eye	E-tox-lo-waw.
Eyebrow	To-do-no-lup-pa-is-see.
Eyelash	Tose-lis-kee.

F.

Face	To-so-faw.
Fan	She-ma-caw.
Fat	Nee-haw.
Father (my)	Solk-go-chee.
Feathers	Shee.
Feed (to)	Hum-bi-oa-lon-es-chay.
Female infant	Hoke-e-to-chee.
Fence	To-hop-kee.
File	E-show-gaw.
Fingers	In-ka-we-sa-kaw.
Fire	Tode-caw.
Fire-wood (burning)	Tock-hot-chee.
First finger	Som-kil-smil-kaw.
Fish	Thla-theo.
Fish-hawk	Hos-cho-kee-waw.
Fishing-pole	Phon-e-o-hop-ee.
Fish-line	Sar-sho-e-faw-caw.
Fish-net	Whe-ah.
Flea	Cuff-ko.
Flour	To-paw.
Flower	Im-pock-pock-ee.
Fly	Tsa-na.

Across the Everglades

Foot	E-lee.
Footprint	Es-tel-e-hop-o.
Forehead	Ka-ho-waw.
Forget	Cha-ho-sit.
Fox	Chil-la.
Friend	His-see.
Frog . . . . . . ˙ . . .	Aw-pa-to-naw.
Frog (Tree-)	Skin-cho-caw.
Front teeth	E-no-tee-ho-maw.

G.

Gall berries	Aw-shit-ta-taw.
Ginger-cake (large)	Tock-a-la-kee-chom-paw.
Ginseng	Hi-lis-hot-kee.
Girl	Hoke-ti-chee.
Give (to)	Ah-mos-chay.
Glass tumbler	Shot-hit-go-chee.
Gnat	Scop-o-swaw.
Go (to)	Hi-e-pus.
Goat	Cho-wa-taw.
Goat (mountain)	E-cho-wa-a-taw.
Good	Hintz-kay.
Goose	A-hak-wa.
Grapes	Chil-loos-wa.
Grasshopper	A-caw-ko-taw.
Gravy	E-po-see-waw.
Gray	Sho-po-ka-hot-ka-chee.
Green	Pi-e-lon-o-maw.
Ground	E-ho-tee.
Gun	Ayt-sah.

H.

Hair	E-caw-e-see.
Hammock	Sho-a-los-ga-taw.
Hand	In-kee.
Hatchet	Po-chos-wo-chee.
Hawk	Sho-caw.
Head	E-caw.

Seminole Vocabulary

Head-dress . . . . Eka-sim-enah-hits-ka.
Hear (to) . . . . Im-po-hos-chee.
Heart . . . . E-fer-caw.
Heaven . . . . In-like-e-taw.
Hell . . . . E-lich-es-caw.
Heron (great blue) . . . . Wak-ko-lot-ko.
Heron (great white) . . . . O-shot-caw.
Heron (little blue) . . . . . Wak-ko-lot-ko-o-hi-lot-tee.
Heron (little white) . . . . O-shot-co-chee.
Hickory-tree . . . . O-chee-o-pee.
Hide (cow) . . . . Wa-ka-haft-bee.
Hip . . . . Im-po-loke-cho.
Hoe . . . . E-sho-e-caw.
Hog . . . . Sok-a.
Hog (wild) . . . . Su-caw-pin-si-law.
Home (my) . . . . Aw-lock-a-taw-chaw-ho-tee.
Hommock . . . . Ez-ee-lo-faw.
Honey . . . . Chum-pee.
Horn . . . . Yi-pee.
Horse . . . . Cha-lok-ko.
Hot . . . . Hai-see.
Hunt (to) . . . . Fi-i-it-lot-es-chee.

I.

I . . . . Annee.
Ibis (white) . . . . Hi-lo-lo.
Ice . . . . It-to-tee.
Ice-hatchet . . . . It-to-tee-butch-es-waw.
Ice-house . . . . It-to-tee-in-so-go.
Ice-machine . . . . It-to-tee-saw-gaw.
Ice-moulds . . . . It-to-tee-ock-les-waw.
Ice-saw . . . . It-to-tee-ish-fo-gaw.
Ice-tongs . . . . It-to-tee-she-lot-caw.
Ice-water . . . . It-to-tee-we-waw.
Indian . . . . Es-ta-chat-tee.
Indian's heaven . . . . . . Po-ya-fits-a.
Infant . . . . Est-to-chee.
Instep . . . . E-lit-ta-pix-tee-e-fa-cho-to-kee-not-ee.

Across the Everglades

Iron . . . . Shot-to.
Iron kettle . . . . Hot-cus-waw.
Island . . . . O-tee.

J.

Jay (blue) . . . . Tos-chee.

K.

Kettle . . . . Alk-us-wah.
Key . . . . Ees-how-ees-caw.
Kingfisher . . . . O-cho-ka.
Knife . . . . Slof-ka.
Knife-belt . . . . She-won-nock-e-ta-sa-lof-kaw.
Knife (dull) . . . . Sa-lof-ka-tof-nee.
Knife (sharp) . . . . Sa-lof-ka-fots-kee.
Knuckle . . . . In-ka-we-sock-ka-e-to-pee.

L.

Lake . . . . Ok-hass-ee.
Lamp . . . . Ko-lo-kee.
Lantern . . . . Ko-lo-kee-e-ho-tee.
Laugh (to) . . . . Op-peel-it.
Leg . . . . Hats-ka-wats.
Leg (above knee) . . . . . Chee-hof-ee.
Leg (below knee) . . . . . Chee-host-go-waw.
Leggings . . . . Aw-fa-tee-kaw.
Lemonade . . . . Yel-la-haw.
Like (to) . . . . Chi-yot-chit.
Limpkin . . . . Ho-shock-e-a-caw.
Little . . . . Chat-kee.
Liver . . . . E-lo-pee.
Living coals . . . . Toke-la-waw.
Lung . . . . In-hee-shock-e-taw.

M.

Maid (old) . . . . E-he-se-ko.
Mallet . . . . Chot-to-go-chee.

Seminole Vocabulary

Man	Es-tee.
Man (married)	E-hi-wa-o-chit-ee.
Man (old)	Ach-o-be-li-tee.
Manatee	E-chos-waw.
Meat	A-pess-wah.
Milk	Wah-ku-pissee.
Minnow	Sar-sho-chee.
Moccasin	Ist-e-lee-pik-kah.
Mocking-bird	O-shi-hi-yi.
Money	Shaw-toke-e-naw-waw.
Moon	Ha-lits-chey.
Morning	Hal-ay-yat-kee.
Morning star.	Hi-yi-tee-e-chaw.
Morrow (To-)	A-pox-see.
Mosquito	O-he-aw.
Moss	Aw-shen-waw.
Mouth	E-choke-o-waw.
Mulberry-tree	Kee.

N.

Naked	E-caw-e-pee.
Navel	E-ho-cho-waw.
Neck	No-ka-pee.
Needle	Ees-la-pode-caw.
Negro	Es-tee-lus-tee.
Night	Hih-lee.
Night (To-)	Mo-shon-nist-lee.
Night (To-morrow)	A-pox-see-nist-lee.
No	Hick-ast-chee.
Nose	E-ho-po.
Nostril	E-po-haw-kee.

O.

Oak	Lok-tsa-sum-pa.
Oak-leaf	Lok-e-tum-ba-e-cee.
Oatmeal	To-lee-ko.
Oats	Til-e-ko.
Onion	Ti-fum-bee.

Across the Everglades

Opossum	Sok-a-hat-kee.
Orange	Il-la-haw.
Otter	O-sa-na.
Otter-skin	O-shon-aw-haft-bee.
Owl	O-pah.
Ox	Wal-ka-ho-non-waw.
Oysters	Whit-lo-ko.

P.

Paddle	Is-kahf-ko-chee.
Paint	Co-lo-waw.
Paint (black)	Co-lo-wa-lus-tee.
Paint (red)	Co-lo-wa-chaw-tee.
Paint (yellow)	Co-lo-waw-la-nee.
Palm (of hand)	In-ko-faw.
Palmetto (cabbage-tree)	Tol-o-lock-o.
Palmetto (seed)	Tol-o-neck-la.
Palmetto (young cabbage-tree)	Tol-o-chee.
Panther	Kat-sa.
Paroquet	Pot-see-lon-ee.
Partridge	Ko-ai-kee.
Peanut	Com-to-lock-o.
Pepper-sauce	Ho-wah.
Persimmon	Shot-taw.
Persimmon (seed)	Shot-o-nin-kla.
Persimmon (tree)	Shot-i-pee.
Pickerel	Shup-sho-chee.
Picture	Es-ti-ha-kee.
Pillow	We-hop-caw.
Pin	Ti-sos-so-chee.
Pine	Choo-lee.
Pineapple	Chili-i-hos-waw.
Pistol	Ta-pate-go-chee.
Plant (to)	Ah-ho-chee.
Plenty	Or-gis.
Poor	Wi-o-kee-tus-chay.
Pot (of pottery)	Le-ho-chaw.
Potato (sweet)	Aw-haw.

Seminole Vocabulary

Potato (white)	Aw-hot-to-pox-to-chee.
Potted ham	Aw-pis-ta-lake-a-to-me.
Pottery	Polk-ko.
Powder	To-ho-to-waw.
Pulse	In-ka-shock-a-tee.
Pumpkin (Indian)	Chos-chee.
Pumpkin (white man's) . . .	Chos-chee-lock-o.
Puppy	E-fa-chee.

Q.

Quail	Fo-a-kee.
Quinine	He-swan-i-hit-caw.

R.

Rabbit	Cho-fee.
Rabbit (gray)	Cho-fee-chaw-hot-ee.
Rabbit (skin)	Cho-fee-haft-bee.
Raccoon	Wood-ko.
Railing	See-la-hot-tit-taw.
Railroad (car)	To-to-lese-pof-a-naw-o-cha-go.
Rat	Ches-she.
Rattlesnake	Chit-ko-la-la-go-chee.
Red	Chat-tee.
Redbird	Fost-chi-taw.
Rib	In-to-law.
Ridge (of nose)	E-po-fa-nee.
Rifle	E-chaw.
Ring	Stink-ko-shot-ti-tee-caw.
Robin	Eash-pock-a-waw.
Rookery	Fo-shon-nits-kaw.
Rump	E-tol-kay.

S.

Sack	Shoke-chaw.
Saddle	O-pa-tock-o.
Saliva	E-to-ka-lo-swa.
Salt	Oke-tsam-wa.
Sardines	Cot-lo-chee.

Across the Everglades

Sausage	Fit-chee.
Sausage (beef)	Wa-ka-fit-chee.
Sausage (pork)	Suck-a-fit-chee.
Sawdust	To-fo-ga-ta-leg-a-mee.
Saw-palmetto	She-hop-paw.
Scalp	Cho-pock-e-taw.
Sea	We-hat-ka.
See (to)	He-ches-chee.
Seine	Wee-aw.
Sell (to)	Yi-co-chay.
Shirt	Hi-ef-cof-ka-taw.
Shoes	Stila-pa-won-hee.
Silkworm	To-ka-tes-kee-at-tee-lo-e-waw.
Silver	Chat-to-ko-na-wah.
Sing (to)	E-hi-e-kit.
Sister	Cho-wen-waw.
Skin	Shon-aw-haft-bee.
Sleep (to)	Sop-pa-lon-es-chay.
Smell (to)	Oh-in-i-it.
Smoke	Eh-cho-chee.
Snake	Chit-to.
Snake (green)	O-co-la-chit-ta.
Snake-plant	Chit-ta-hum-pe-ta.
Snake (spotted)	Chit-ta-lock-a-chee.
Snipe	We-hot-ko-fo-sho-wo-chee.
Soap	So-cose-caw.
Sole (of foot)	Es-tel-e-ho-faw.
Son (my)	Sop-po-chee.
Soup	O-po-swaw.
Sour	Ka-mok-see.
Space (between knuckles)	In-ko-yock-pee.
Sparrow-hawk	Sho-ko-chee.
Spider	Och-klo-kow.
Spider-web	Och-o-klon-we-ahr.
Spring	We-waw-ese-pay-lot-caw.
Squash	Tahai-ah.
Squirrel	E-thlo.
Squirrel (red)	Klo-hi-lee-chaw-tee.

Seminole Vocabulary

Squirrel (gray) . . . . Klo-hot-go-chee.
Stomach . . . . Im-pa-shaw.
Stove . . . . Tode-ca-e-ho-tee.

T.

Tail . . . . E-hot-chee.
Teeth . . . . E-no-tee.
Throat . . . . Sin-no-ka-nil-caw.
Thumb . . . . Som-kit-kee.
Thunder . . . . Ti-nit-kee.
Toad . . . . Ko-tee.
Tobacco . . . . Hee-chee.
Toe (large) . . . . Es-tel-e-eeds-kee.
Toe (nail) . . . . E-la-ni-ka-so-swaw.
Toe (second) . . . . Es-tel-e-nock-clay-ho-e-claw.
Tongue . . . . To-los-waw.
Toothpick . . . . Ees-ti-no-tee-some-fo-tee-taw.
Towel . . . . In-ka-e-to-shi-eets-caw.
Town . . . . Tolo-fa.
Trunk . . . . To-how-ho-waw.
Turkey . . . . Pen-na-waw.
Turkey (beard) . . . . . . Pen-na-waw-en-to-wee.
Turkey (cry) . . . . Pen-cha-ho-gaw.
Turkey (gobbler) . . . . . Pen-ni-chaw.
Turkey (hen) . . . . . . Pen-nit-kee.
Turtle . . . . Lot-sa.
Turtle (land) . . . . Lo-chaw.
Turtle (soft shell) . . . . . Ho-lock-wa.

U.

Upper eyelid . . . . Tode-le-waw-hos-pee.
Upper lip . . . . Choke-hos-pon-a-paw.

V.

Valise . . . . To-hi-o-waw.
Village . . . . Cho-co-ta-ti-yee.
Vulture . . . . Sho-lee.
Vulture (black) . . . . . . Sho-lee-pee-los-pes-ko.

Across the Everglades

W.

Wagon	Tose-to-lese-taw.
Walk (pavement)	Ho-low-paw.
Wash-pavement (bowl)	Ho-e-so-clope-pa-lock-a-naw.
Water	We-wa.
Water-lily	Shil-o-fo-haw.
Water-tank	We-wa-ho-tee.
Weed	Aw-tock-claw.
Whang (for sewing moccasins)	To-shay-sil-caw.
Whippoorwill	Chip-ee-lop-law.
Whisk-broom	Sin-ti-ne-ta-pi-ee-to-caw.
Whiskey	Y-o-mee.
Whistle (to)	Tote-ca-taw.
White	Hot-ka-tee.
Whooping-crane	Wa-to-law.
Widow	E-hi-lift-mus-chee.
Widower	E-hi-wa-se-ke.
Wild	Ho-nit-chay.
Willow-tree	Aw-won-aw.
Wolf	Yee-haw.
Woman	Hoke-tee.
Woman (old)	Hoke-tee-li-tee.
Wood (to burn)	E-to.
Worm	U-e-cot-taw.
Wrist	In-tee-ti-pix-tee-e-toke-kee-tay-gaw.

Y.

Yesterday	Pox-son-gay.
Young (man)	Ho-non-wa-mi-nit-ti-tee.
Young (woman)	Hoke-tee-ti-mit-nit-ti-tee.

Months.

January	Ho-ti-lee-has-ee.
February	Ti-sot-to-chee.
March	Ti-sot-to-lock-o.
April	Kee-hos-ee.

Seminole Vocabulary

May . . . . Got-so-hos-ee.
June . . . . Hi-yote-chee.
July . . . . Hi-yote-lock-o.
August . . . . Ti-ose-go-chee.
September . . . . Ti-ose-go-lock-o.
October . . . . E-ho-lee.
November . . . . Si-lof-slop-ko.
December . . . . Si-lof-so-kee.

Numerals.

One . . . . Hum-kin.
Two . . . . Ho-ko-lin.
Three . . . . To-che-nes.
Four . . . . Os-tin.
Five . . . . Chaw-kee-bin.
Six . . . . A-pa-kin.
Seven . . . . Ko-lo-pa-kin.
Eight . . . . Chin-na-pa-kin.
Nine . . . . Os-ta-pa-kin.
Ten . . . . Pa-lin.
Eleven . . . . Pa-lin-hum-kin-hum-kin.
Twelve . . . . Pa-lin-hum-kin-ho-ko-lin.
Thirteen . . . . Pa-lin-hum-kin-to-che-nes.
Fourteen . . . . Pa-lin-hum-kin-os-tin.
Twenty . . . . Pa-lin-ho-ko-lin.
Twenty-one . . . . Pa-lin-ho-ko-lin-hum-kin.
Twenty-three . . . . . . Pa-lin-ho-ko-lin-to-che-nes.
Thirty . . . . Pa-lin-to-che-nes.
Forty . . . . Pa-lin-ostin.
Fifty . . . . Pa-lin-chaw-kee-bin.
Sixty . . . . Pa-lin-a-pa-kin.
Seventy . . . . Pa-lin-ko-la-pa-kin.
Eighty . . . . Pa-lin-chin-na-pa-kin.
Ninety . . . . Pa-lin-os-ta-pa-kin.
One hundred . . . . Chope-kee-hum-kin.
Two hundred . . . . Chope-kee-ho-ko-lin.
Three hundred . . . . . . Chope-kee-too-chin-ee.

Across the Everglades

Sentences.

A great deal	Stu-es-taw.
All gone	Suc-chay.
All sit down	A-pok-es-chay.
Are you sleepy ?	Che-mo-on-ot-es-chay.
Bird cry	Hoc-es-chee.
By and by	Aw-tee-tus-chee.
Come here	He-a-maw.
Deer walk	E-cho-wak-op-po-sit.
Don't know	Kit-lix-chay.
Do you hear ?	Im-po-hitch-caw.
Give me money	So-toke-kee-na-aw-mun-chee.
Glad to see	Ha-tee-e-tew-chee-hick-chay-hit-es-chay.
Good-by	Ay-lip-ka-shaw.
Good luck	Som-mus-ka-lar-nee-shaw.
Good wishes to white man	Som-mus-ka-lar-nee-sha-maw-lin.
Green corn dance	Shot-cay-taw.
I am lost	Chi-ho-ches-chee.
I can't find it	He-chos-kos-chay.
I saw deer run	E-cho-lid-kit-he-chus-chee.
I saw deer walk	E-cho-yac-op-po-sit-hi-chus-chee.
I take	Sup-pa-lon-es-chay.
I will grow tall	I-ti-it-tot-chi-mi-he-taw-mi-he-taw-te-hee.
Let us go	I-hoo-es-chay.
Let us hunt	Lop-fi-ets-chay.
Lie down and sleep	No-chit-pay-lon-es-chay.
Like them	Chi-yot-chit.
Long time	O-fun-net-taw.
Many come	I-wox-chee.
Me too	On-e-wa.
Mother wants to keep him .	Its-kee-e-i-chee-tok-naw.
My knife is long	Sa-lof-ka-chop-kaw.
Sit down	Li-kus-chay.
Sit down on steps	Hi-top-cay-ta-li-kus-chay.
Sit on floor	To-pa-li-kus-chay.

Seminole Vocabulary

Sun come up	Ha-sha-i-sit.
Sun gone down	Ha-sha-col-lok-tit.
To pole a boat	Che-to-gaw.
To put moccasins on	Es-tel-e-pi-e-ka-u-cha-ko-ot-e-he.
To row a boat	Scof-gaw.
Wash hands	In-ka-o-ko-sit.
Water rough	Im-e-lo-la-tee-ti-yee.
What is it?	Nok-a-tee.
Which way?	Stom-a-taw.
Wind blew hard	Is-chay-to-ma-es-chee.
You eat plenty	Hum-bug-a-chay-hum-pee-taw.
You lie	Lox-a-dox-chay.

INDEX

Index

Index

Index

Index

Index

Index

Index

THE END.

DE SOTO'S MAP

IN THE "HAMMOCK"

DR. TIGER

MATLO

BILLY STEWART AND HIS BRIDE
(Showing Indian attire)

MIAMI DOCTOR'S BOY

THE MOUTH OF THE MIAMI RIVER

COCOANUT GROVE

POST-OFFICE AT CUTLER

FOWEY ROCKS LIGHT-HOUSE

SOLDIER KEY

ON SOLDIER KEY

CROCODILE HUNTING

THE HAUNT OF THE CROCODILE

THE CROCODILE AT HOME

BREWER ON KEY LARGO

THE CRAW FISHERMEN

A FOUR-POUND CRAWFISH

THE LOOKOUT FORWARD

CAPE SABLE BEACH

COCOANUT-TREES NEAR THE SHORE

ON CAPE SABLE

ALONG THE COAST

THE "CUPID" IN HARNEY RIVER

THE EDGE OF THE EVERGLADES

THE NOONDAY REST

OUTLOOK FROM STATION 2

MAKING CAMP

OUTLOOK FROM STATION 3

FILLING THE CAMP BUCKET

A MERIDIAN ALTITUDE

ON WILLOUGHBY KEY

A GOOD CAMPING ISLAND

IN THE BIG SAW-GRASS

A GOOD WATER-LEAD

STATION 8

SLOW TRAVELLING

OUTLOOK FROM STATION 9

SHOAL WATER OVER ROCKY BOTTOM

TWO INCHES OF WATER OVER ROCK

OUTLOOK FROM STATION 12

LOOKING FOR LAND

EASTERN EDGE OF THE EVERGLADES

THE RAPIDS OF THE MIAMI RIVER